MARISA MELTZER

GIRL POWER

Marisa Meltzer is the coauthor of *How Sassy Changed My Life* (Faber and Faber, 2007). Her work has appeared in *The Wall Street Journal*, *Slate*, *Elle*, and *Teen Vogue*. She attended the Evergreen State College and now lives in Brooklyn, New York.

How Sassy Changed My Life (coauthor)

GIRL POWER

GIRL POWER

THE NINETIES REVOLUTION
IN MUSIC

MARISA MELTZER

FABER AND FABER, INC.

AN AFFILIATE OF FARRAR, STRAUS AND GIROUX

NEW YORK

FABER AND FABER, INC.
An affiliate of Farrar, Straus and Giroux
18 West 18th Street, New York 10011

Copyright © 2010 by Marisa Meltzer
All rights reserved
Distributed in Canada by D&M Publishers, Inc.
Printed in the United States of America
First edition, 2010

Library of Congress Cataloging-in-Publication Data
Meltzer, Marisa, 1977–
    Girl power : the nineties revolution in music / Marisa Meltzer.— 1st ed.
        p.   cm.
    Includes bibliographical references and index.
    ISBN 978-0-86547-979-1 (pbk. : alk. paper)
    1. Riot grrrl movement.   2. Women rock musicians.   3. Women in
popular culture—History—20th century.   I. Title.

ML82 .M456 2010
781.64082'09049—dc22

                                                        2009025435

Designed by Abby Kagan

www.fsgbooks.com

1   3   5   7   9   10   8   6   4   2

CONTENTS

PREFACE

The phrase "girl power" is not about to win any popularity contests. When I polled friends, associates, and perfect strangers about those two seemingly innocuous words, no one seemed to identify with it. I got dismissive answers such as "boring," "faddish," "trivial," and—my personal favorite—"a catchphrase for an MTV special or a *Seventeen* article and not a subject for a substantive discussion." Despite the term's implied feminism, much of the criticism comes from strong advocates for women's rights. "On the long list of things that are bad for feminism," wrote Rachel Fudge in the anthology *BITCHfest*, "Phyllis Schlafly, *Girls Gone Wild*, pharmacists who refuse to fill birth-control prescriptions, to name a few . . . girl power would hardly seem to be the most pernicious. And yet as one of the most visible contemporary manifestations of the vague idea of feminism, it earns a special place of loathing in this feminist's heart."

I totally get it. One of the most ubiquitous phrases of the nineties, "girl power" is Generation X's version of the cheerful seventies slogan "Well-Behaved Women Seldom Make History," which reduced any of the social and political gains of the women's movement to a mere catchphrase. Its empowerment seems limited to the power to consume. It's tailor-made for baby tees (another ubiquitous nineties fashion cum political statement) or tubes of lip gloss. It's feminism reduced to the shallowest choices and devoid of collective action.

Some people hear "girl power" and immediately think of the apocryphal sisterhood sold by girl groups like the Spice Girls. But, in my mind, the two words reflect both a feminist message and a changing feminism. Girl power encompasses the story of music and feminism over the last twenty years. Women's place in music has changed drastically in that time, and while some of this happened underground, some of it was very mainstream.

If one thing is a given, it's that counterculture movements become commodified and the underground becomes the mainstream. The rebellious women of punk took on a shinier hue with new wave, which became friendlier still with the feminist-flavored pop singers of the 1980s. Riot grrrls' rage begat the more media-friendly Hole and Babes in Toyland, then the more muffled discontent of Alanis Morissette. The radical, separatist Michigan Womyn's Music Festival birthed Lilith Fair. The Spice Girls paved the way for the much tartier Pussycat Dolls. There wouldn't be a Britney or a Miley without Madonna and Cyndi Lauper. It's easy to dismiss each iteration as less authentic than the last—the classic indie-snob trope of "There was this great moment, but you're too late to revel in it." But the music industry is one very visible microcosm of the way women's roles have changed radically in the last two decades.

Girl power's staying power prompted my curiosity, and I realized that in order to account for what's happened in music—and in pop culture at large when it comes to women—I needed to understand it. So in this book I have traced the roots, evolution, and eventual co-optation of girl power in an attempt to figure out what it all means and where music and feminism are headed.

Music is my entry point, partly because "girl power" is a phrase associated foremost with music, but also because music has been a defining part of my own life. Music is often most important to you when you're really young or really pissed off. Luckily, in the nineties, I was both. My timing was right; there was a place in the culture for all my adolescent rage. It was an era that was unapologetically political—engaging issues like third wave feminism, gay rights, safe sex, and environmental activism. And being political wasn't code for "boring"; it was actually cool after the more politically dormant eighties.

The nineties was a watershed decade for music made by (and often for) women, and the culmination of a long history of girl bands. Bands that were unabashedly feminist, that made angry and challenging music—music that would have been relegated to the underground in the eighties—became mainstream. I'm not the only one who noticed. "A revolution came through music in the nineties," Megan Jasper, the executive vice president at Sub Pop Records, told me. "The beginning of the decade was the beginning of cultural change. Mainstream, normal people were open for something different. Those are rare moments and it felt like a cultural shift in a lot of ways."

I lived many treasured clichés of the decade, complete with the standard-issue indie-rock tale of being rescued from life as an apathetic suburban teenager by riot grrrl, the feminist punk movement. I cut my hair short, wore YOUR BODY IS A BATTLE-GROUND buttons on my backpack, and engaged in all-girl sing-alongs to "My Red Self," the early riot grrrl band Heavens to Betsy's ode to menstruation. The story of girl power kicks off with riot grrrl, but this isn't a book just about riot grrrl, or even the nineties. It's also a book about how everything that happened afterward was just as, if not more, important: how an underground movement trickled up from punk-rock utopias to teen girls' bedrooms around the world. Riot grrrl didn't stay within the confines of one scene, which allowed the concept of girl power to grow into something much larger and, I think, more interesting.

This book will have a narrow and highly selective focus by design; it's a discussion and an analysis as viewed through the lens of personal experience. Following my own taste and personal history, I have chosen to focus mostly on the genres of pop and punk. The good feminist in me wants to make sure I'm not overlooking any outsider groups, but they are not part of the story I'm looking to tell. I hope I'm only beginning a conversation, which could and should be had with other genres, such as hip-hop, metal, or country music. This book is by no means a definitive roster of women in rock music—there's a chance I left out your favorite band (and I'm still waiting for Madonna's publicist to return my calls!). But I am thrilled that so many musicians were eager to sit down for an interview, including members of Bikini Kill, the Raincoats, Rainer Maria, the Indigo Girls, Galaxie 500, Mates of State, and the Blow, to name-drop just a few.

Chasing girl power took me from Madison Square Garden, where I watched Beyoncé and her fifteen-piece all-girl band play to a sold-out crowd, to rural Michigan, where I camped (and confronted my innate distrust of singer-songwriters) at the Michigan Womyn's Music Festival. I saw fledgling tween bands with names like the Pink Devils and XX Chromosomes play their first

guitar solos at the Willie Mae Rock Camp for Girls. I saw Pink
sing about the scourge of celebutantes in "Stupid Girls" to a sold-
out arena and M.I.A. and her hypewoman play "Boys" while a
gaggle of girls sang along and danced onstage. I became one of
Hannah Montana's most geriatric fans and preregistered for tick-
ets to the Spice Girls reunion.

While girl power might be empowerment-lite, it's not going
away. When a movement transitions, it doesn't lose all its po-
tency. Instead, it leaves us with pop infused with politics. This
book is a way of assessing our worn-out copies of *The Immaculate
Collection*, our milk crates of limited-edition Huggy Bear seven-
inches, our WHAT WOULD JOAN JETT DO? T-shirts, our wrinkled
ticket stubs to Lil' Kim at the Colosseum, our Hard Candy lip
gloss, and our *Glitter*/*Crossroads* double-feature viewing parties.
Girl power is, as Professor Alison Piepmeier says of her own
10,000 Maniacs– and Suzanne Vega–obsessed college years, about
"seeking a culture of women's voices. I knew I had things to say
and I wanted to find women who were making a public space for
themselves." Girl power allows each of us to map out what it
means to be a woman in the world, one song at a time.

GIRL POWER

1

RIOT GRRRLS

The Evergreen State College in Olympia, Washington, is the kind of university that offers neither grades nor majors. Its central quad is called Red Square; its concrete-block, riot-proof buildings are nestled among acres of forested land; and the chili in the main café is always vegan. As can be expected from its left-of-center reputation, the school has attracted a mix of outcast students since its inception in 1967: hippies, slackers, and punks. It's also my alma mater. And I count myself as one of them.

Olympia is the capital of Washington State. It's small—the population only about forty thousand—and some of the only decent jobs available to graduates who want to stick around are for the state government. But it was (and still is) cheap enough that a bohemian existence can be fairly easily cobbled together with part-time day jobs conducive to the lifestyle of a fledgling band. In the mid-eighties, an all-ages punk scene cropped up in the city, buoyed by a club called the Fabulous Tropicana; the student radio station KAOS; the music fanzine *Op*; and Calvin Johnson's label, K Records, and his band, Beat Happening.

To a certain kind of person, the Olympia lifestyle could seem ideal. The musician Tae Won Yu moved there from his native New York City in the spring of 1992 because it felt like "a paradise. I woke up every morning feeling like, 'I can't believe I'm in Olympia. It's like Paris in the thirties.'" The singer Mirah Zeitlyn describes early nineties life in Olympia: "We were all making rock operas and we had this huge theater we could use when we wanted. There are certain kinds of energy that maybe can't be replicated." Naturally, she organized her college music collection not alphabetically or by genre, but by gender. "I didn't think twice about it. Sometimes I want to listen to this stuff that men make and sometimes I want to listen to this stuff that women make."

The Olympia musician Lois Maffeo grew up in the cultural doldrums of Phoenix, Arizona, and heard about Evergreen through a high school friend who was being hassled by her hippie uncle to go there. "I was like, 'No grades? I'm so sold,'" she recalls. Maffeo had a by-the-books college paradigm shift: her first dorm mate was a punk girl with dyed blond hair and raccoon-like makeup. Calvin Johnson of Beat Happening helped Maffeo learn the guitar by drawing her a three-chord chart and saying, "People have done worse with more." She went to art shows at a space called Girl City and hosted a radio show of music entirely made by women called *Your Dream Girl* on KAOS. "I locked into the fact that girls just run this town," said Maffeo. "Going to an all-girl high school, there wasn't that constant trying to vie for the attention of boys. I felt like girls were rad. I didn't need to be convinced." The writer Mikki Halpin lived in Los Angeles but knew the town by reputation: "There were a lot of people who really would make a very convincing claim at that point in time that Olympia was a matriarchy."

On the other side of the country, Washington, D.C., was a city known for its punk bands. It was also where Calvin Johnson had lived during high school. He had befriended many of the bands in D.C., and in the years after he moved back to his native Olympia to attend college, a kind of cultural exchange developed between the underground music scenes in the two cities.

In 1991, Maffeo was living in D.C.'s Mount Pleasant neighborhood when riots broke out following the shooting of a Salvadoran man by a black female police officer who had been trying to arrest him for disorderly conduct during a Cinco de Mayo celebration. "They went on for days. You'd run home from the bus stop hoping not to get hit by anything," says Maffeo. Watching the physical confrontation between a community and the police was oddly energizing, she remembers. "We realized you can push back, it's okay. It really was an exciting feeling." One day during the riots, her housemate Jen Smith ran into the house and said, "What we need is a girl riot."

The idea of starting a girl gang or a girl riot had been percolating since punk's inception. The sixties and seventies had seen a wave of fierce female musicians who sang about their lady experience (meaning the whole spectrum the good, the bad, the ugly—of women's lives) in a manner that was far more matter-of-fact than any music that had come before. Women like Janis Joplin, Grace Slick, Joni Mitchell, Carly Simon, Carole King, Stevie Nicks, and Suzi Quatro achieved a level of success, some becoming household names, beyond being the muse or the groupie. Others, like the women's liberation bands—utopian feminist music collectives founded across the United States that wrote songs with titles like "Abortion Song," "Ain't Gonna Marry," and "Papa Don't Lay That Shit on Me"—achieved a certain feminist notoriety. Yet mainstream rock remained resolutely, with some notable exceptions, a boys' club. The album had evolved into an art form in and of itself in the sixties, with albums like the Beach Boys' *Pet Sounds* and the Beatles' *Sgt. Pepper's Lonely Hearts Club Band*. Rock was about virtuosity and, unless you're a diva, virtuosity has always been associated with being male. By the seventies, rock music had become a bloated and long-winded affair—look no further than prog bands like Yes and Genesis. And if writing twenty-minute opuses or incorporating lasers and flying pianos into their live shows was too manly, the guys could always just spurn it all for the gender ambiguity of glam rock—a movement that gave men a lot of room to play with their sexuality while still managing to leave little place for women. Women were so shut out as cultural creators that even when femininity was valued, men were still the vehicle.

Enter punk, a movement that rejected technical virtuosity and professionalism in favor of amateurishness, iconoclasm, and a do-it-yourself aesthetic. Punk gave a generation of boys who didn't fit the All-American Boy Scout type a new blueprint for masculinity and a license to be whatever they needed to be. Punk gave girls who never felt at home in the bows and dresses and canopy beds of traditional girlhood a new way of being female. Because musical skill wasn't the point, it leveled the playing field, encouraging young women to join bands, get onstage, and learn to play as they went—even in front of audiences. It also wasn't about singing nicely or quietly. During the late seventies, the women of punk were creating a new female archetype, borrowing notions of collective community responsibility from the women's liberation movement and, at the same time, taking the utmost pride not just in individuality but in being an outcast. The Slits, an all-girl punk band from London, disparaged normal female roles in their song "Typical Girls," asking "Who invented the typical girl?/Who's bringing out the new improved model?/And there's another marketing ploy/Typical girl gets the typical boy."

Ana da Silva spent her teen years listening to the Beatles and the Rolling Stones in Portugal, where she grew up. She moved to England for college just as punk was beginning. "That informed the way I did things. People were saying it was so easy to start a band," she says. She began to go to shows around London, formed her own band, the Raincoats, and got to know the women in other bands, like the Slits. But she still found a certain amount of pigeon-holing among women in that scene, where all-girl punk bands were still more obscure than their all-boy counterparts. "We did get put into a bag. We were always compared to the Slits whereas the biggest similarity was that we were actually women."

Sharon Cheslow grew up in the D.C. area and, as a teenager in the late seventies, learned about punk from the pages of *Seventeen* magazine, *The Washington Post*, and *Creem* magazine. The music was similar to the rock she had loved in the sixties—simple and lacking the overwrought theatrics of the arena rock that dominated the radio—and she was drawn to its musicians. "I saw images of the women who were gender benders. That's what really caught my eye. These were women who were not afraid to say, 'We're not traditional women and we're going to create in a way women aren't encouraged to create.'" Even in punk's rejection of gender norms, it was relatively rare to see an all-female band. After seeing the Mo-dettes—a girl punk band from London formed by one of the original members of the Slits—at D.C.'s 9:30

Club, Cheslow went to talk to the singer, Ramona Carlier. "I'll never forget the advice she gave me. She said, 'You can't deny the fact that you're a woman, but the most important thing is to focus on creating music.'"

Cheslow had been encouraged to take up guitar by her folk-music-loving parents, but couldn't find anyone to play music with because none of the boys her age wanted to be in a band with a female electric guitar player. "When I first started playing guitar, I really felt like I could be one of the guys or for the guys. I rebelled against that. I wasn't interested in joining some other culture—I wanted to create my own culture. That's what punk had taught me, that I should be free to create as a girl. Not to support a guy or be one of them, but to be respected by the guys." By the early eighties, she had started Chalk Circle, the first all-girl band in D.C.

Even though punk had made many inroads for women, it was rarely disputed that there was room for improvement. Punk may have been a source of liberation for some women, but it wasn't always explicitly feminist. Patti Smith, the most famous woman to emerge from New York's nascent punk scene, which was led by bands like the Ramones and Television, had always allied herself with men rather than supporting a sisterhood. She didn't hesitate to disavow the feminist movement as a whole, telling one interviewer, "I ain't no women's-lib chick." There were only a few token women in punk, and to identify themselves as feminists would only make their non-maleness more central—it was hard enough just being accepted as a musician.

It's also possible that the women's liberation movement was too mainstream for the outsider women of punk. The rise of punk rock was happening at the same time as the second wave of feminism in America. Feminism's so-called first wave was a movement christened retroactively, referring primarily to the late-nineteenth-and-early-twentieth-century fight for women's suffrage. The second wave of American feminism began in the early sixties and focused on social and legal rights, like the legalization of abortion and equal pay. Solidifying events like the birth control pill being approved for marketing in 1960, the formation of the National Organization for Women in 1966, 1968's demonstrations against the Miss America pageant, the first women's studies courses being taught at Cornell University, *Roe v. Wade* legalizing abortion, and the 1972 passing of Title IX (which made discrimination by sex illegal for any government-funded educational program or activity) all happened during the second wave's sixties and seventies heyday. The women's liberation movement always harbored radicals at its fringes, but as it became an established part of American politics, perhaps it wasn't cool enough for the underground.

Sexual harassment, one of the issues around which the second wave sought to create awareness, was alive and well in the punk community. When Chalk Circle played shows, men in the audience would wolf whistle, yell at them to take off their clothes, call them bimbos, or resort to the tired adage that they were "good for girls." After the first influx of punk in the late seventies, which had some degree of gender parity, the scene had grown increasingly macho. Heather Lewis's gender was a source of constant comment for people who saw Beat Happening, her early eighties band with Calvin Johnson and Bret Lunsford. But the Olympia trio was already something that, as Maffeo tells it, "made people mad." People who saw them were irked that the band didn't, at least in a conventional sense, rock; it lacked a bass player and wrote songs about rabbits and bananas. While the band rotated instruments, Lewis mainly played the drums and, as the only girl, would frequently be the subject of hecklers at shows. "Some guy would yell, 'Nice flannel shirt. Are you a lesbian?'" says Maffeo.

Slowly, a space for gender discourse was forming. Maffeo watched Lewis take on her hecklers firsthand. "That's a situation where so many would crumple, but she would not break stride. She'd say, 'You sound like you've got some emotional problems.' She would take it slow, defuse the situation, and she wouldn't yell back. She would think about it for a second and answer them really calmly. You couldn't defy the power of that moment." In D.C., there had been attempts to address sexism in the local punk community, which had become nationally known with the success of bands like Minor Threat on the Dischord Records label. Cheslow, Cynthia Connolly, Amy Pickering, and Lydia Ely organized discussion groups to talk about women in punk for a 1988 issue of the seminal punk zine *Maximumrocknroll*. At the same time, both men and women in the D.C. scene were becoming increasingly aware of issues like sexual harassment and rape. In 1990, Fugazi, a D.C. band that was arguably one of the most well-known and respected indie bands in the country, wrote the song "Suggestion" from the point of view of a woman. "Why can't I walk down the street free of suggestion?/Is my body the only trait in the eyes of men?"

As it became more common for girls to form bands, go on tour, or release records, a network of girls in the punk scene was developing not just in D.C., but across the country. It was a community that wasn't just based on playing an instrument; many of the women were also writers or activists. It's no coincidence that this was a group of women either in or recently graduated from college, with memories of their first radicalizing moments still fresh. As *Bitch* magazine's cofounder Andi Zeisler points out,

"You're at the age where militancy is paramount, like when some-one takes a women's studies class and realizes, 'I'm not the only one who's bummed out when my boyfriend asks me to hold his jacket when he goes into the mosh pit.'" Rather than waiting for the playing field to become level, women were realizing that they could start their own league. For Cheslow, it was a relief to see younger girls questioning many of the same things she had dealt with years earlier. "By then I had given up playing in bands. I had actually gotten too discouraged. It was too much of a battle for me being this lone female guitarist and I got burnt out." Hanging out with them gave her the sense that they looked up to her as someone who had been through it before. "To have these girls with this fighting spirit, who thought you shouldn't give up, it renewed my own spirit," she remembers. "It gave me so much energy that it's lasted to this day."

So by 1991, when Jen Smith called for a girl riot, the time was ripe for women in punk to band together. Tobi Vail, an Olympia native, was in an all-girl band in high school called Doris and in another band with Calvin Johnson, the Go Team, in the late eighties. In the fall of 1990, her latest project was a band called Bikini Kill with Kathleen Hanna, Billie Karen, and Kathi Wilcox. "One of the ideas we were working with in Bikini Kill was that if girls started bands, it would transform culture and not just empower them as individuals, but change society. It would not just put them in a position of power, but the world would actu-ally change. As a young girl who was frustrated by a lack of women in music who called themselves feminists, I saw a need to change that."

These women were reacting to issues within the relatively in-sular punk community, but also tapping into a larger cultural moment. The late eighties had been a particularly dark moment for feminism, and the decade became a kind of grab bag for feminist gains and losses. *Time* magazine's "Women Face the '90s" story, published in December 1989, featured a cover image of a woman with a baby in one arm and a briefcase in the other. The text read, "In the '80s they tried to have it all. Now they've just plain had it. Is there a future for feminism?" This story came just a few years after the coining of the term "postfeminism" to describe a new generation of women benefiting from the gains of the women's liberation movement. The vogue for the word was disheartening—the prefix of "post" implied not only that all the work of feminism had been accomplished, but that feminism itself was passé.

The generation of women that followed the second wave had reaped the benefits but were coming of age on their own and beginning to critique the past twenty years. Third wave feminism was both a resurgence and a reaction to the second wave. Third wave feminism was about embracing the individual, and acknowledging that feminism could be different for everyone, and was not some monolithic force. Its core texts—Rebecca Walker's 1991 *Ms.* story "Becoming the Third Wave" and two other books that came out that same year, Naomi Wolfe's *The Beauty Myth* and Susan Faludi's *Backlash: The Undeclared War Against American Women*—struck huge chords for young women seeking to define their own brand of feminism. The ideas behind the third wave, which might once have been sequestered in the underground or on college campuses, were converging and often breaking through to the mainstream. Nineteen ninety-two was the inaugural year of the Ms. Foundation's Take Your Daughter to Work Day (known more inclusively since 2003 as Take Your Daughters and Sons to Work Day). "Even the Girl Scouts of America was rethinking its approach to girlhood with updated literature and a newfound focus on finding your voice and self-esteem issues," says Lyn Mikel Brown, a professor at Colby College who studies media and marketing to girls. "It felt like an exciting moment." Activism was everywhere again, whether it was the Rock the Vote campaign to encourage young voters to become politically active, Take Back the Night rallies on college campuses to protest campus rape, ACT UP and Queer Nation raising AIDS awareness in the gay community, or the Million Man March on Washington for the black community. Riots made headlines not just in Mount Pleasant but also in Los Angeles after the verdict in the Rodney King trial.

Soon after the Mount Pleasant riots, Tobi Vail, Kathleen Hanna, and their like-minded friends Allison Wolfe and Molly Neuman of the band Bratmobile collaborated on a new zine (a handmade, self-published magazine) called *Riot Grrrl*. Vail transfigured the word "girl" to "grrrl," giving it a ferocious growl. (The original spelling of "grrrl" with three Rs became the official terminology, though it was often misspelled as "grrl" or, worse, "grl.") "We really did sit down and say, 'How can we change what it means to be a girl?' and 'How can we reinvent feminism for our generation?' and we actually came up with a plan and then implemented it," Vail says. Bikini Kill published a two-page manifesto preaching their own brand of feminist uprising—what they called "Revolution Girl-Style Now." The manifesta urged girls to "resist psychic death," "cry in public," join bands, teach one another how to play instruments, and fight back against both possible aggressors and the Man.

From Bikini Kill's eponymous zine in 1991:

Riot Grrrl is:
BECAUSE we know that life is much more than physical survival and are patently aware that the punk rock "you can do anything" idea is crucial to the coming angry grrrl rock revolution which seeks to save the psychic and cultural lives of girls and women everywhere, according to their own terms, not ours.

BECAUSE we are angry at a society that tells us Girl=Dumb, Girl=Bad, Girl=Weak.

BECAUSE I believe with my wholeheartmindbody that girls constitute a revolutionary soul force that can, and will, change the world for real.

The musician Rachel Carns, who lived in Olympia during the riot grrrl years, said in an interview for a riot grrrl retrospective at the Experience Music Project in Seattle, "Girls have this private thing about themselves—diaries, your room—that is really isolated and you don't share it with anybody else." In a way, riot grrrl sought to link these individual bedrooms and to make modern girlhood less of an isolated event to endure. Riot grrrl was one of the last youth movements that existed before the widespread use of the Internet. Just a few years later, girls would be able to easily connect to other like-minded teens via very public diaries in the form of blogs and, later, social networking sites. But in the early nineties, making connections took some work.

One early riot grrrl influence was the 1981 cult classic film *Ladies and Gentlemen, the Fabulous Stains*, whose plot revolved around a group of angry teenagers who start an all-girl punk band. It wasn't a story seen onscreen very often. In one of the movie's iconic moments, the snarly lead singer, Corinne "Third Degree" Burns, played by a pubescent Diane Lane, pronounces that "every citizen should be given an electric guitar on her sixteenth birthday." The film became an oft-named inspiration for many women in music in the nineties. In particular, it left a mark on riot grrrl, whose bands owed a debt to the Stains, not just aesthetically but in spirit as well. (With nostalgia for the nineties so rampant these days, Rhino, the company that released the film on DVD, is smart to use the Stains–riot grrrl relationship to their marketing advantage: Tobi Vail is even quoted on Rhino's website saying that the movie is "the most realistic and profound film I have ever seen.")

As a platform for girls to connect, riot grrrl owed a debt to an even earlier generation. "The most important thing about this music, the reason it spoke to us so powerfully," writes Susan Douglas in *Where the Girls Are*, "was that it gave voice to all the warring selves inside us struggling, blindly and with a crushing sense of insecurity, to forge something resembling a coherent identity." Douglas is talking about the girl groups of the early sixties like the Shirelles or the Crystals, but she could just as easily be discussing the female sense of community in listening to Bikini Kill or Bratmobile. "They knew things about boys and love that they shared with each other, and this shared knowledge—smarter, more deeply intuitive, more worldly wise than any male locker room talk—provided a powerful bonding between girls, a kind of bonding that boys didn't have," Douglas writes.

Riot grrrls spoke frankly about issues adolescent girls faced that the larger culture didn't want to talk about. This included some subjects previously considered too dark or taboo, such as incest, rape, and eating disorders. Sharon Cheslow had moved to San Francisco in 1990, but moved back to D.C. for the summer of

1991, partly because she was so inspired by the riot grrrl scene there. She played in a short-lived band with Hanna called Suture. "These were not issues talked about in rock songs," she says. Even though punk had long been about embracing taboos, these were issues that weren't being addressed, possibly because they were the domain of girls. Riot grrrl encouraged girls not to be passive cultural consumers, but to create zines or bands themselves. Fittingly, some riot grrrls started to hold meetings loosely modeled after the consciousness-raising groups of the seventies.

But while there were plenty of ties to their mothers' generation of feminism, there were also some key differences. As any woman who grew up listening to "William's Doll" on the *Free to Be You and Me* sound track or who wasn't allowed to play with Barbie knows, second wave feminism had long held a derisive attitude toward the more frivolous aspects of girlhood. In the seventies and eighties, good feminists were women—sometimes spelled with a Y—and they mostly listened to womyn's music, which seemed earnest or serious or angry, and impossible to separate from associations with the smell of nag champa. Being a woman was about being an organized grown-up who worked, two traits usually foreign to the rebels and creative types who created pop music. Betty Friedan and her cohorts may have grooved to the poppy "I Am Woman" at the closing ceremonies of 1973's NOW convention, but Helen Reddy's hit is the exception to the rule; in pop music, girls always end up outnumbering women.

Riot grrrl's chosen moniker of "girl" (never "woman" or—shudder—"gal") was not meant as infantilization, but as a nod to their joyous youth. In the early eighties, the Harvard psychologist Carol Gilligan published *In a Different Voice*, her groundbreaking book about girls and self-esteem. In it, she posited that when girls are little, they are true to their beliefs, speaking their minds and getting angry. They're confident, they're proud of being different, they're happy to resist authority. According to Gilligan, girls go through a crisis of confidence at puberty; their self-esteem plummets, and they never truly recover. She thinks that this is because America views boys as the norm: girls are different, and their way of being in the world isn't validated by society at large. Reflecting girls' concerns—with parents and boys and having fun—is affirming who they are and what they are interested in, and it is an inherently feminist act.

A 1997 article on girl power in *The Village Voice* noted that "riot grrrls had seen firsthand, through their mothers, that being a grown woman involves making awful choices and sacrifices. Whereas girls still had all options open to them—none of life's roads were blocked off yet." The second issue of the *Bikini Kill* zine featured the words "girl power" on its cover. "As far as I know, the term 'girl power' didn't exist before Kathleen and I made it up," notes Vail. "I can't remember exactly what the circumstances were, but I am pretty sure I thought of it and told Kathleen, and then she made a flyer that said 'girl power' on it, and then we both started using the term a lot in our writing and in conversation with people." Girl power was both a nod to Gilligan's theories and an embrace of all the candy-colored frivolity of girlhood. Girl power married the optimism of their pre-adolescent years with the sense of activism and, sometimes, rage that they felt as adults. It was a phrase riot grrrls were fond of: a T-shirt the British riot grrrl band Huggy Bear made for a tour with Bikini Kill read TOTALLY GIRL POWERED.

Riot grrrl was first and foremost about making punk rock a more hospitable place for girls—that was the only requirement. But it also came in a cutesy pink package, complete with a wholehearted embrace of child-style objects previously verboten to good feminist women. Grrrls wrote zines filled with essays decrying the term "prick tease," made collages of women cut out from vintage ads, and cooked vegan recipes.

Riot grrrls were infamous for their sartorial choices, perhaps because that aspect of the movement was easy for the press to latch on to. They had a penchant for dressing up like anarchist school-girls, pairing plaid Catholic school kilts, knee socks, pageboy haircuts, pigtails, barrettes, and baby tees with ripped stockings and combat boots. With riot grrrl, you could enjoy the playful aspects of being a girl and want to fight the power at the same time. It wasn't uncommon to see SLUT or RAPE or WHORE scrawled in Sharpie marker across a riot grrrl's belly, the intended idea being self-objectification—taking what you imagine sexist guys in the audience are saying to themselves, and confronting them with it. They were heavily loaded, often ironic symbols, but symbols that nonetheless created a gulf between their feminism and their mothers'. "It was a way to keep those tangible comforts of our childhood and still test the waters as card-carrying women," says Beth Baldwin, an indie-music fan who was in college in western Pennsylvania during riot grrrl. In retrospect, she concedes that she maybe regrets the baby barrettes a bit, the intention being pure, but the perception possibly coming across a little warped. "It was never sleazy," Baldwin notes. "It felt true and pure to who we were." It also gave Generation X feminists a uniform immediately discernible as different from the Birkenstocks, turquoise jewelry, and long hair of their mothers. Stacy Forte, a veteran of the New York City music scene, had a shaved head and wore big Doc Martens boots in the early nineties; her idea of a feminist was "someone who was as tough as a man." When she discovered riot grrrl, she loved that "all these girls were girly enough to carry handbags and wear lipstick but were still tough. It seemed like a higher form of feminism, to embrace girliness and throw it in everyone's faces rather than trying so hard to be macho."

Years later, after moving to upstate New York, Forte joined an all-women potluck group that meets once a month. The women who come range in age from their twenties to their seventies, and most of them are organic farmers or entrepreneurs of some kind. "I think that the spirit of riot grrrl really affected how I understood all-female spaces," she says. "I know for most of the women in the group, the women-only thing probably feels more connected to the nineteen seventies. But for me it's totally riot grrrl." Girl-only spaces were a way for riot grrrls to confront the fact that culture often meant "male culture" and that anything by a woman was going to be labeled for women, creating a kind of pink ghetto. "I think it's politically important to assert a difference, to ridicule and expose the operation of this othering," says Julia Downes, a member of the British riot grrrl scene. To her, it's saying, "I recognize that my art, music, writing, and culture has been historically denied from its rightful place, and I want to fight for visibility in connecting with this past as well as supporting other women doing the same things."

Riot grrrl was girl power at its most brash and unfiltered. It created the most uncompromising (and defiant and audacious) female persona in music in recent history. There's a classic photo of riot grrrls at a pro-choice demonstration in front of the Supreme Court in 1992. Amid all the dour activists, one twenty-something girl stands out. She is wearing a flowered bikini top and a pair of cutoffs and has RAPE scrawled across her belly in what looks like lipstick. Her sign says, KEEP YOUR FIST OUTTA

MY CUNT. It was the aggression mixed with femme style that gave riot grrrl its edge; Beth Ditto, the singer for the Gossip, a post–riot grrrl punk band originally from Olympia, called riot grrrl "the first time in history valley girls were feared." But all of this must be taken with the caveat that, however legendary in reputation these bands were among women's studies majors and in the punk scene, they certainly never cracked the Top 40.

Mirroring the fashion contradictions, riot grrrl songs would alternate between wailing and singsong melodies. Alternating between quiet and loud wasn't a new musical trope—the Pixies had built a career doing it in the eighties—but, from the mouths of riot grrrl singers, it felt like they were interrogating the very state of girlhood. When Hanna sings in "Feels Blind," an early Bikini Kill song in which she bellows, "As a woman I was taught to always be hungry/yeah women are well acquainted with thirst/ we could eat just about anything/we'd even eat your hate up like love," it was, for many fans, like they were hearing their inner lives represented in a song for the first time.

When interviewed for a 1996 story about rock music and feminism in *New York* magazine, the singer Liz Phair said that the act of watching a woman rock out onstage is, for teenage girls, "like having someone in a movie that you can follow. It's like having a character you can live through. And for so long, they didn't. You go to a rock show because you want the guy to stare at you. You want to be noticed and singled out as an object. And this time, they are watching someone and pretending they are her. And that's a very good experience, I think, for the self-esteem of the young American girl."

On seeing Bikini Kill play for the first time, the former Heavens to Betsy and Sleater-Kinney singer Corin Tucker has said, "It was the first time I'd ever seen feminism translated into an emotional language. That I saw those kinds of thoughts and ideas put into your personal life . . . For young women to be doing that, basically teenagers onstage, to be taking that kind of stance, that kind of power, was blowing people's minds. And it totally blew mine." The way she tells it, it was akin to what seeing the Ramones play live did for would-be punks: Bikini Kill inspired budding women musicians to do it themselves and form their own bands. Says Tucker: "I was like—okay, that's it. That's it for me— I'm going to start a band, right now. You had the feeling they had started the band the week before: you can do it too."

But it wasn't just young musicians who embraced the culture of riot grrrl; established musicians found inspiration in the movement too. While touring in the early nineties, Amy Ray from the Indigo Girls (a queer folk duo from Georgia who had won mainstream success in the late eighties with their songs "Closer to Fine" and "Galileo") started to receive zines from girls about, as she describes them, "body image or classism or rape or all sorts of crazy dark poetry—all these things you deal with." She saw her band as being somewhat isolated from the folk and feminist music scenes, touring but keeping to themselves. Between the zines and hearing more and more bands fronted by women, it convinced her that there was a community of young, outspoken feminists out there. Her all-girl British punk band the Raincoats had been dormant since the eighties, but seeing riot grrrl made Ana da Silva enthusiastic about making music again. "They were inspired by us and we got inspired by them."

In the summer of 1991, K Records held a weeklong International Pop Underground Convention in Olympia. Nirvana had been slated to perform but ended up touring Europe with Sonic

Youth instead. Of the fifty bands playing the festival, the ones with the most widespread popularity were probably Beat Happening and the Glaswegian band the Pastels. Resolutely independent, its program promised, "No lackeys to the corporate ogre allowed." It was a galvanizing moment for women in that scene; a group of all-women bands performed together on a girls' night called "Love Rock Revolution Girl Style Now," organized by Molly Neuman and Allison Wolfe, whose band, Bratmobile, played along with Lois Maffeo, Heavens to Betsy, Suture, and 7 Year Bitch.

Maybe the best part about riot grrrl was that it wasn't, at its outset, celebrity focused. Its geographical centers, D.C. and Olympia, weren't exactly cultural capitals, and one didn't need to be friends with, say, the girls in the Olympia riot grrrl band Excuse 17 to experience it. In those pre-Internet times, word spread through the punk community via zines, letters between pen pals in far-flung music scenes, and bands going on tour. And riot grrrl bands had sprung up around the world—Emily's Sassy Lime in California and, in England, Skinned Teen and Huggy Bear. A riot grrrl network emerged in cities like New York; Portland, Oregon; Chicago; and Los Angeles, where high-school- and college-aged girls held their own riot grrrl meetings, during which members talked about subjects ranging from sexual harassment and body image to zine distribution and putting on shows. By the summer of 1992, there was even a riot grrrl convention in D.C., featuring workshops, spoken-word poetry, concerts, and an "All-Girl All-Night Dance Party." It was ultimately a scene connected through not just ideals but songs and so many zines, in fact, that in an early story on riot grrrl in a 1992 edition of *LA Weekly*, Emily White referred to it as "an underground with no Mecca, built of paper."

There were plenty of young women, primed on messages they had never heard before about the power of girls, who were ready to embrace riot grrrl. Issue eight of the zine *Scruffy* declared, "I am an ugly oppressed freaky punk girl and so of course I'm a feminist and of course I'm a Riot Grrrl." The music writer Hannah Levin transferred to the University of Washington in Seattle in September 1991. "I was in a perfect storm. I landed there and riot grrrl was starting to completely explode." So much so that she arrived at school thinking she was going to major in creative writing, but instead "after all my years of denial that I was a feminist, I became a women's studies major." The writer and photographer Maria Sciarrino and her friends, who were teenagers looking for something to emulate, used to delight in writing SLUT across their bellies, just like the riot grrrls they saw in magazines. "We were from suburban New Jersey looking for dates for the prom, so I'm not sure we were really riot grrrls," she admits.

The writer Mairead Case grew up in Seattle in the early nineties in the wake of the death of Mia Zapata. Zapata had been the singer of the Gits, a band that, while not riot grrrl, certainly came from the same Pacific Northwestern punk milieu and shared some of the same ideals. In the summer of 1993, Zapata was raped and murdered while walking home from a Seattle bar. The aftermath of her death brought renewed interest in self-defense among women in the punk community all over the country. Riot grrrl, for Case, embodied all of that. "At some point, even in a basement in Olympia, you could be like, 'This is my cellulite, don't rape me, fuck off.'"

At the time of the rape and murder, Shayla Hason, a DJ and photographer, was attending Evergreen's unofficial sister school, Antioch College, where the Gits had formed. (The school became famous—and widely mocked—for its sexual offense policy requiring explicit verbal consent between partners, though as Hason helpfully points out, at school it didn't actually "stop anyone from having orgies or getting laid.") She thinks that riot grrrl moved her to a kind of naive confidence that allowed her to deal with catcalls from men on the street by intensely confronting them. "I would totally freak out on these forty-year-old guys, some on crack, saying, 'Do you think I'm going to ask for your phone number? What the fuck, man?' And me, at five-three with glasses and combat boots—it made me stand up for myself. I knew I didn't have to take it. Riot grrrl gave me the strength to do that." When she was the only girl in a show of forty artists at the Lower East Side's Alleged Gallery, she asked the gallery owner, Aaron Rose, to paint the back of her motorcycle jacket with the words RIOT GRRRL in carnival-style lettering. Later the jacket made an appearance in her parents' temple's version of *Grease*.

Jen Hazen was a riot grrrl fan in college in western Pennsylvania. "I'm sure part of it had to do with being in college, but I don't know if I've ever felt so much excitement at something new, while at the same time being allowed so much free artistic rein with just my life in general." She started a zine called *If the Shoe Fits* that was, like many riot grrrl zines, partly about music and partly about herself. In terms of music, she says, "Bikini Kill and Bratmobile just nailed the kinetic energy, the momentum that had built up after years of backlash and progress, backlash and progress."

I was a suburban teenager whose life was changed by riot grrrl. I didn't have any siblings to be my personal ambassadors to good music, and so I was someone who benefited from riot grrrl's media onslaught—I read about it in *Sassy* magazine. I can't think of anything more exciting to my nascent feminist fourteen-year-old self than photos of girls in halter tops, torn fishnets, and smeared red lipstick. They weren't much older than I was but already had bands and manifestas of their own. At a time when I was dying to differentiate myself from my *Ms.*-reading, Phoebe Snow–obsessed mom, and boys scared me so much that the easiest thing to feel toward them was resentment, riot grrrl felt like the answer.

I soon became a convert. After seeing Bikini Kill my junior year of high school at the all-ages club 924 Gilman Street in Berkeley, California, I realized I was the only girl with long hair and cut mine short. When I was bored in physics, I wrote "revolution girl-style now" over and over again in my notebooks, the way besotted girls are supposed to doodle the names of their crushes. I mail-ordered copious records from labels like Kill Rock Stars, K, Chainsaw, and Villa Villakula, and read zines with names like *Girl Germs*, *Teenage Gang Debs*, and *Gunk*. My northern California high school had an entirely student-run radio station, and my show was called the *Secret Teenage Radio Riot*. When guy friends whose car cassette players I hijacked would complain to me about how tuneless Heavens to Betsy sounded, I felt sorry for their cluelessness. Everything about riot grrrl felt like it was speaking directly to me, and I thought they sounded exactly like it felt to be a seventeen-year-old girl. I was hooked.

Granted, riot grrrl wasn't a panacea for teenage woes—it didn't help me understand the mysterious world of boys at all, and all the body empowerment it preached couldn't have saved me from a protracted eating disorder. But at a vulnerable stage it did make me feel like I had ownership of something that was just for me. I never heard of, let alone attended, an actual riot grrrl meeting, and I didn't have very many close friends at my high school. I was fairly awkward at meeting people at the concerts I did go to—even though, in retrospect, I imagine that we were a crowd full of girls wanting, at least on the surface, the same things—but they did make me feel like there was a place where some core part of me would be understood.

It's particularly embarrassing to admit this, but I went to college in Olympia at least partly because of riot grrrl superfandom. The city seemed like the utopia of third wave feminism I was looking for. During my undergraduate years, I lived out all my high school fantasies. I sang along to Sleater-Kinney's "Dance Song '97" at parties, and I even played in a band called the Skirts that performed all its music on toy instruments. The thing that seems to impress people the most from those years is that I lived downstairs from Kathleen Hanna. She was exceedingly patient with me, considering I semi-stalked her, constantly asking to borrow glue or sugar, all too eager for any chance to talk to her.

But I wasn't the only one to give her the hero-worship treatment. "This is probably the best thing I have or will ever get in my life," began a blurb in a riot grrrl zine, *MTM*. "I am considering calling the man/boy/guy/male who gave it to me a god." The manna from heaven? A chunk of Hanna's black hair, which is photocopied into the layout with a hand-lettered note and arrow proclaiming, "This is the hair."

Riot grrrl may have put on airs that it was ultimately about doing it yourself and that it had no centralization and no leader, but all movements have leaders, whether they actively claim the mantle or are simply anointed. Both the press and young would-be riot grrrls looked to Hanna as the face of riot grrrl and of third wave feminism, christening her the next generation's Gloria Steinem. "I was resented by certain people because I was getting attention that they weren't getting, even though I didn't ask for it and I never talked to the press," Hanna has said. It's a position she's resisted and tried to distance herself from in the years since (right up to declining to give an interview for this book).

"If you can get up on stage and take your clothes off," Hanna, herself a former stripper, once said, "performing a punk show is nothing." In concert, she sometimes came across as a punk parody of Madonna, appearing onstage in a bikini top or biker shorts. She was even rumored to have invented the cryptic title of the defining nineties anthem, Nirvana's "Smells Like Teen Spirit." Kurt Cobain was a friend of Hanna's and she scrawled the joking reference to the deodorant Teen Spirit—which was unavoidable at the time, prominently featured in embarrassing, faux-hip advertisements—on the wall of his Olympia home. But while she may have inspired the song that catapulted grunge to the mainstream, she also wrote what was for some the decade's most infectious anthem, Bikini Kill's "Rebel Girl." It's a song that the former Rainer Maria singer Caithlin De Marrais followed along with to learn to play bass and that tween bands cover on YouTube. Alongside songs from Motörhead and the Grateful Dead, it's even on the popular play-along video game *Rock Band 2*, where hopefully it's winning over a second generation of fans.

Pop music has long held girls' heterosexual love for boys as the central relationship and theme, but "Rebel Girl" subverts the formula. In it, cool is identified as another girl. And for once, it's not about getting a guy's attention. The lyrics—"Rebel girl/you're the queen of my world/I think I want to take you home/I want to try on your clothes"—evoke what friendship and fascination between girls is really like. And it takes insults that could be lobbed at the subject and turns them into the crux of the singer's adoration—"That girl thinks she's the queen of the neighborhood/I got news for you—she is/they say she's a dyke/but I know/ she's my best friend." The idea of sisterhood accrues additional power in songs like "Rebel Girl" because riot grrrl bands knew their songs would be sung back at them by a room full of like-minded women. (And since the token guys in the audience were usually relegated to the back of riot grrrl shows, it really did look like a mass of girls.)

Every self-respecting riot grrrl band had a girl anthem. Huggy Bear declared in "Her Jazz," "This is happening without your permission/The arrival of a new renegade." In the song "Girl Germs," Bratmobile revels in the idea of its own toxicity to boys: "You're too cozy in your all-boy clubhouse/to even consider having Kool-Aid at my house," sings Allison Wolfe. In the heyday of AIDS, the "girl germs" of the song's chorus relate to girls' self-protection and their ability to block unwanted sexual advances. According to Joanne Gottlieb and Gayle Wald in their essay "Smells Like Teen Spirit: Riot Grrrls, Revolution and Women in Independent Rock," " 'Germs' here also suggests 'germinal,' the potential girls have to develop into powerful women; alternatively, it refers to girl-specific culture in its embryonic stages."

Documenting your scene was a common mandate in punk. And it was important in riot grrrl especially, notes Calvin Johnson, "so girls in the future will know you came before them." To the mainstream media, a bunch of angry but still sexy twenty-something women was irresistible, and they were quick to descend upon the scene. *Sassy*, *Newsweek*, *USA Today*, *LA Weekly*, *Seventeen*, and the British music weekly *Melody Maker* all wrote early stories on the movement in 1992 and 1993. Producers from the talk show *Sally Jessy Raphael* were rumored to be calling around, trying to get a real-life riot grrrl to take on the dinosaur rocker David Lee Roth (unfortunately, no one rose to that challenge). The hit sitcom *Roseanne* even had a riot grrrl plotline in which Roseanne and Jackie, two of the show's main characters, pick up a riot grrrl hitchhiker (played unconvincingly with long nails and heavy makeup by the actress Jenna Elfman) who's in a band called the Unit Shredders and gives them a Bikini Kill cassette tape. "There's a revolution going on we don't even know about," says Roseanne. *Newsweek* called it "feminism with a loud happy face dotting the 'i.'" *USA Today* wrote in an equally patronizing tone that "from hundreds of bedrooms comes the young feminist revolution. And it's not pretty. But it doesn't wanna be. So there!"

Andi Zeisler was living in Italy during the height of riot grrrl and found out about it through the British music press, where *Melody Maker* wrote that "the best thing that any Riot Grrrl could do is to go away and do some reading and I don't mean a grubby little fanzine." The *Daily Star*, a British tabloid, took an especially alarmist slant: "They screech, they spit, they snarl, they swear. Every word they scream through the microphone is a prayer against men . . . They are the toughest, meanest group of feminists since women began burning their bras in the swinging sixties." Zeisler remembers that those articles—maybe even without meaning to—were really good at pointing out the sexism in the music industry. "They would get letters from people who were like, 'These girls suck, you're just covering them because they're cute.'" The American music magazines were no better. *Rolling Stone*'s article was called "Grrrls at War"—pitting bands or notable girls in the movement against one another was a common trope in the mainstream media. Of course, there were rumors of alleged rivalries between certain women in the scene, but the message of riot grrrl was supposed to be about changing feminism for young women, not supporting a stereotype as tired as catfighting.

At least one magazine let the grrrls speak for themselves. Bratmobile's guitarist Erin Smith interned at *Sassy*, the unabashedly feminist, indie-obsessed teen magazine whose brief publication coincided with riot grrrl. Smith eventually became the magazine's "Washington bureau chief," a job that consisted partly of writing dazzlingly insidery reports on the D.C. scene for the magazine's half-million teen readers. But even that sort of fawning attention wasn't unilaterally embraced by all riot grrrls. "Not only did *Sassy* seem like it was for rich, preppy, private school girls, but it was upwardly mobile and embraced pop culture and a lot of traditional femininity I had been taught to reject," says Tobi Vail. "Basically all the things I had spent my entire adolescence defining myself against—capitalism, girliness, entertainment." She concedes that she read *Sassy*, albeit with ambivalence. "It was so confusing to find them writing about my friends—and later me—because I was young and I felt they were from a different social group, people who would have hated me in high school for not liking new wave or not shaving my legs or washing my hair or wearing a bra." Still, *Sassy* was riot grrrl's most earnest and consistent mainstream supporter.

The women of riot grrrl were right to be suspicious of the media's glare. Tobi Vail, who had dated Kurt Cobain, had seen firsthand the negative things that could happen when the media latches on to your story. And in most of the articles, they were made to look like ridiculous girls, angry or punch-drunk on their first taste of feminism. It helped that the grrrls were hot and scantily clad—the media was particularly keen on capitalizing on the interest that the general (male) reader might take in the riot grrrl's sexy "bad girl" image. What the media didn't understand was how tongue-in-cheek so many of the riot grrrl accoutrements were—no one cared whether you had on the right spiked belt or knee-high socks or owned the complete Bratmobile discography. The girls who tended to be attracted to riot grrrl felt like they had the higher calling of rescuing girls' lives and identities and trying to restore the self-esteem of women at a young age. They were tired of being portrayed, as Corin Tucker has said, as "ridiculous girls parading around in our underwear." The core message of riot grrrl was about finding one's own voice, and to then see the media trying to interpret that for you could be deeply disconcerting. "It was such a creepy time period for the mainstream media," says Tobi Vail's sister, Maggie. "They co-opted everything and they eventually co-opted riot grrrl."

The voracious interest in this underground subculture came down to timing. By the early nineties, the distinctions between what was underground or alternative culture and what was mainstream went from blurry to more or less indecipherable. The runaway success of Nirvana heralded a media interest in almost anything hailing from the Pacific Northwest, and riot grrrl was poised to be the next big thing.

Another part of the problem with the press was of nomenclature—there was little differentiation between riot grrrl bands and bands that simply had women in them. Riot grrrl's Bikini Kill, Heavens to Betsy, and Bratmobile certainly weren't the only groups with strong women in them in the early nineties—there were plenty of bands, like L7 or Babes in Toyland, who were like-minded and also from the punk community but didn't use the term to describe their music or philosophy.

Zine editors rose to the defense of the movement. The zine *Starache* published a rather earnest examination of riot grrrl over several issues in the mid nineties that takes on its newfound coolness, the media, and the world at large:

> i know that it has been twisted to mean different things (a certain fashion, boy haters, and other stupid shit) and that there are a lotta girls in it just cuz it is cool . . . you don't have to attend meetings, to be a riot grrrl, you don't have to listen to bikini kill, you don't hate boys. it comes from within. it is kind of like what punk means to me. it is a set of beliefs. unfortunately both punk and riot grrrl are being fucked up by the media right now but it won't last.

The riot grrrls did court some of the media. Jennifer Baumgardner, coauthor of *Manifesta: Young Women, Feminism, and the Future*, was an intern at *Ms.* magazine in 1992 and was feeling the feminist generation gap. "I didn't yet know how to distinguish myself from what came before me, so I had to pretend like their issues were my issues," she says. "I'd be like, 'Yeah! Wage discrimination!' Except that wouldn't be an issue for me because I worked in an all-women's workplace." So she was relieved when Kathleen Hanna called the *Ms.* office and said to Baumgardner, "I care about *Ms.* so I will come to you, I'll bring the mountain to Mohammed." But even the feminist magazine of record wasn't jumping at the chance to cover the movement. Baumgardner eventually convinced the editors that it was worthy of mentioning. "I think if it was left up to *Ms.* there would have been no connections ever made to riot grrrl, because, even though they really respected their interns, there was a way in which they didn't take those sort of suggestions seriously." While riot grrrl rejected the mass media, at least the mass media latched on to the importance of the movement, even if missing out on a nuanced understanding of it. But the feminist establishment wasn't ready either, making riot grrrl a marker of a new wave—and a new generation of feminists who were challenging the ideology of second wave feminism.

In the fall of 1992, just a few months after *LA Weekly* ran its feature story on riot grrrl and other publications were rushing to publish their own accounts, the women of riot grrrl declared a media blackout. They decided that the mainstream media was taking too large a role in defining what riot grrrl was, so bands, zine editors, and riot grrrl organizers simply stopped cooperating with outsiders en masse. "Because we had all been talking about how power is manifested in society, well if we want to change that, then how can we take some of that power back?" Cheslow has said. "So one of the ways that we decided to take power back . . . was to put a ban on the media."

Tobi Vail worked at Kill Rock Stars part-time as the mail-order person and, ostensibly, the receptionist. Since almost every call would be someone from the media asking to speak with someone from Bikini Kill, the solution had been simply to never answer the phone. That's where Maggie Vail came in. Maggie was happy to pick up the phone and deal with the media, though it was a strange first experience for handling the press. "I would have to say, 'Sorry, *Rolling Stone*, *Time*, *Spin*, Bikini Kill can't talk to you,'" she recalls. Other bands on the label made up of all boys were jealous of the attention and would whine to her about how happy they would be to talk to a glossy national magazine. The media blackout was never called off but riot grrrl still thrived, albeit in a smaller, more grassroots version: bands still put out records and toured, zines were still produced, riot grrrl chapters were still maintained.

By the time of the blackout, the media's backlash against riot grrrl had already begun. In 1992, the journalist Evelyn McDonnell moderated a panel called "The F-Word" that included Kathleen Hanna and Bratmobile's Erin Smith during the annual CMJ (*College Music Journal*) Conference in New York. "It was one of the few times when a lot of us women got together in a really public place and talked about those issues. I was ridiculed in *The Village Voice* for having done it and I really felt like that was the start of some of the backlash against riot grrrl and feminism," she explains. "Riot grrrl was too political for indie rock and 'the code word for "political" was "boring."'"

The media blackout was a rash move and something that seems more baffling in a post-Internet age accustomed to constant coverage. "I never thought the media ban was a good idea," says McDonnell. "It was too defensive of a move. They felt like they were under attack and they retreated. When you're in battle, you have to keep fighting." "The thing about social phenomena is that they start out really idealistic and beautiful but it becomes about weird control issues," says Calvin Johnson. "It doesn't matter what they write about. If there's a picture of Allison Wolfe, some kid is going to say, 'That's it. I want that' and it's going to change their life. To block out the media is to cut off the nose to spite the face." Reverse snobbery can still be elitist; the predominantly white East and West Coast, urban- and college-town-dwelling riot grrrls forgot about their sistren living in places that didn't have built-in music scenes or a feminist presence, who might have found the message just as useful.

The appropriation of counterculture by the mainstream isn't a new phenomenon. "It's inevitable that the mainstream will look to the underground for sources of ideas and inspiration," says Gayle Wald. "Trying to live out some fantasized notion of purity is always dangerous. It never exists and it's a problematic ideal." To use riot grrrl as an example, its investment in cultural purity caused the movement to turn to policing in the form of the blackout. Or, as Wald phrases it: "It's hard to define what pure looks or sounds like. One person's purity is another person's messiness. And that's okay. A little bit of messiness can allow for some fluidity in a movement."

That first flush of college activism doesn't often make it far post-graduation, when you have to get on with your life. Like many organized groups, riot grrrl quickly became hard to manage and, perhaps, the blackout came at a time when the movement itself was becoming more and more narrowly politicized. Lois Maffeo saw a growing polarization between two factions: the women who were involved for political reasons (discussing identity politics, organizing benefit concerts) and the ones interested in personal gain (making sure their band or zine was popular). Being a riot grrrl was an inherently political act, and one could want to take part in the movement both for the feeling of belonging and for the activism. Punk rock has never purported to be about central stars, so showing any interest in the spotlight was frowned upon. The early nineties in America was a time of increased celebrity—actors replaced models on magazine covers, Madonna's self-obsessed documentary *Truth or Dare* was a hit in theaters in 1991—and the women of riot grrrl certainly can't be faulted for being a product of their own culture. These issues were never resolved, because after the blackout, the movement felt increasingly diffuse and the original riot grrrl bands started breaking up by 1994.

But does a youthful movement that sneers at the dominant cultural paradigm have any room to grow up? It's obvious that riot grrrl is a thorny topic for the girls who were involved in its inception. Some of them shy away from discussing it, remaining loyal to the media blackout decades later. And even when talking about it, parsing the subject is hard. "It is very difficult to look back on," says Tobi Vail, who is still playing in bands. "There was a difference between how we saw ourselves and how we were perceived and what we were trying to do and what actually happened. My view of it now is clouded by everything that came after it. My experience of having named and initiated so much stuff that meant one thing to me personally, and then came to mean another thing in the culture at large, is really difficult to describe." She's talking about the sensation of seeing yourself and your friends and words you invented in the pages of *Newsweek* and *Rolling Stone*. "On the one hand, there's the matter of having a historical legacy to claim (or not claim) and feeling embarrassed and nerdy about that. On the other hand, it's the fear of not being able to move on," says Vail.

The whole scene surrounding riot grrrl was fairly cliquey. Even though "Every girl's a riot grrrl" was a common refrain on stickers, the irony was that, despite the inclusivity preached, there was, as in many subcultures, a clear divide between insiders and outsiders. In that sense, riot grrrl managed to duplicate some of the more tragic aspects of mainstream girl culture, including something that second wave feminism suffered from as well—the feeling that there are popular and unpopular girls. Despite being in college at Evergreen during riot grrrl's inception, it took Mirah Zeitlyn some time to take part. "I have always been awkward at joining groups. My coworker was like, 'There's this new group meeting up called riot grrrl. It's women being empowered and strong.' I didn't feel like I looked right, or dressed like the kind of person who would be at that meeting. I didn't feel empowered enough to go to the meeting."

This cliquishness was only worsened by the fact that most girls attracted to riot grrrl were alienated teens living through heightened angst over fitting in. It's no wonder I cut off all my hair after seeing Bikini Kill play; I wanted to be seen as just as cool as all the short-haired girls in the audience. Every movement has its queen bees and wannabes, and even then I knew exactly where I stood. Immersing myself in the subculture of riot grrrl during my high school years made me lose all interest in some of the hallmarks of high school social oppression, like the prom or homecoming. But in some ways, it provided me with a parallel universe for adolescent hell. I'm grateful I grew up with riot grrrl, but it didn't shield me from adolescent social trauma. I just experienced it at all-ages shows instead of at school dances.

No self-respecting feminist who lived through the nineties wants to come out wholly against riot grrrl. "I never thought that I saw the passionate uproar that I would read about in the media, so I just was never quite sure if it was as inspiring to people as I was being told it was," says the writer Mikki Halpin. As Henry Owens, a musician who was involved with San Francisco's Epicenter collective, where many riot grrrl zines were sold and shows took place, put it: "Here's where I get into trouble. I was really turned off by riot grrrl. It felt like a big reactionary wah-wah session." When pressed to define "wah-wah session," she points out the infantilization—the baby talk, the baby doll dresses, the constant mention of childhood. That was a problem for Courtney

Love as well, who was quoted as saying that she "saw this little riot grrrl in *Spin* who was holding a little magazine called *Princess*. She's fifteen, but everything in her little riot grrrl world—like Hello Kitty products—is telling her to act like she's seven. That's not feminism, it's cultural anorexia."

The writer Cortney Harding was a teenager during riot grrrl. She discovered feminism after hearing Kurt Cobain talk about Susan Faludi in an interview and summarily read her book *Backlash*. She had liberal parents but grew up in a conservative suburb in Oregon and went to a typical high school where athletes were the most popular. Riot grrrl could not have come at a better time. "I bought the concept hook, line, and sinker," she says. "I wore baby dolls and barrettes, wrote on myself, all of it. After striving to be popular in middle school, discovering riot grrrl gave me license to not give a shit, become an activist, put on pro-choice benefits, and generally be a loudmouth badass." But as liberating as all of that felt in the mid-nineties, the feeling didn't sustain her in adult life. "I think riot grrrl did promote an ethos that was unavailable in real life, especially when it came to sexual politics." Writing WHORE on your belly as a sixteen-year-old is empowering in its promotion of sexual freedom. It's a grand gesture that betrays the dogmatic impulses of most teenagers, and foregrounds taboo subjects and misogynist epithets. But what it doesn't do is allow a lot of space for parsing what being a pro-sex feminist means in the world at large. Riot grrrl succeeded at drawing attention to the sexual desires of teenage girls, but gave them little indication of how they should deal with that energy.

Another problem was that as widespread as riot grrrl may have endeavored to be, it was still a movement started largely by and for white, middle-class women. Writing a zine or playing in bands were the main ways to participate in riot grrrl. This meant that you had to live in a culture where you were encouraged to be creative and given lots of help with it—which meant that you had the benefit of good schools and teachers, or parents who valued music or writing. You would then have to have access to zine-making tools and the means of distribution, or music lessons and equipment. These issues of social and economic class weren't unique to riot grrrl, but they weren't aided by the media ban and inherent elitism, either. The fact that the movement was so concentrated on college campuses meant that it attracted the very young—the name alone might have turned off potential converts who felt aged out of girlhood—and the educated.

Gayle Wald got involved with riot grrrl when she was in graduate school in New Jersey, volunteering at a radio station in Princeton. She eventually went to riot grrrl meetings in New York City partly for personal interest and partly to write about it. "When I look back on riot grrrl, one of the tensions was always about class and race. It was something that primarily attracted middle-class women and girls. Even if they weren't living with middle-class incomes, those were the backgrounds." Leah Lilith, a zine editor, has written, "I was coming to realize that the reality of [riot grrrl] groups was far less than their reputation, and much of the time they did not understand or respect my colored girl, leather-dyke, femme, survivor self." What happens in a musical subculture will inevitably reflect American race and class relations, and riot grrrl's problem wasn't whether or not it was open to women of color—it resolutely, desperately wanted to be—but whether its message was of interest to them. That, coupled with the economic and educational barriers, meant that riot grrrls were, by and large, white girls.

Riot grrrl, like feminism, punk rock, or any number of movements and subcultures, did not overthrow the patriarchy. But that doesn't discount its importance—and isn't an effective means of judging its success. "It was one of those tiny things that had incredible power," says Wald. "Every year I meet eighteen- and nineteen-year-olds who still want to talk about riot grrrl"—some of whom were infants when the first riot grrrl zines were being photocopied. "That says something." Of course, girls who aren't in the top rung of their high school's social hierarchy will always have zines (or, more often now, blogs) and bands to turn to. Baumgardner, the feminist writer and former *Ms.* staffer, likens the followers to the radical feminists of the sixties—"there weren't that many of them, but their impact was great." "I'm trying to resist the inclination to write off these movements," says Professor Alison Piepmeier. "These small interventions into hegemonic structures are significant. Any structure that has constant power over people has to constantly reinvent itself, which means that there are always spaces for intervention. Maybe it's at the level of the individual, maybe it's local change."

So maybe the legacy of riot grrrl—as a feminist movement, as a revolution within punk rock, and as a musical harbinger for the rest of the decade—is best understood in other ways. Scientists talk about the butterfly effect—the notion that a butterfly's wings flapping in one place can create tiny changes to the atmosphere that could ultimately cause a massive weather system farther away. Riot grrrl had a butterfly effect on nineties girl music. In other words, before we could have girl power, we had to have revolution girl-style now.

2.

ANGRY WOMYN

When I was fifteen years old, in the spring of 1993, I went with my best friend, Anitra, to the Cow Palace, an arena near San Francisco, to see some of our favorite bands play: Nirvana, L7, the Breeders. It was a benefit concert for the rape victims of Bosnia-Herzegovina, and while I'm sure that not every member of the capacity crowd was there for the politics, I remember feeling excited that such a huge concert was staged for feminist purposes. If riot grrrl had allowed itself to grow beyond the self-imposed limits of underground culture, I wonder if it could have looked something like that night, with Kathleen Hanna singing "Suck My Left One" to a crowd of thousands instead of Kurt Cobain singing "Rape Me." Instead, it boycotted the media and, in turn, the media lost interest.

As the Bosnian benefit showed, riot grrrls weren't the only angry women in rock in the early nineties. Six months before the blackout began, the media was already set to anoint a new crop of bands as the "new she-rebels," to borrow a phrase from a February 1992 article in *The New York Times* by the music critic Simon Reynolds. In it, he identified an emerging movement of hard-rocking women—not riot grrrls, but contemporaries who were disgruntled women nonetheless. The bands profiled were Minneapolis's Babes in Toyland, and Hole and the Nymphs, both from Los Angeles. They were all bands that he posited were poised to become the female equivalent of Nirvana. Reynolds bestowed upon them the rather uninventive moniker of "angry women," mirroring the most popular, if misguided, perception of feminists in pop culture. Ann Powers, then a music critic at *The New York Times*, wrote in February 1993 that "a new round of artists has emerged to challenge the usual virgin-vixen-bimbo stereotypes. L7's androgynous grunge stands out from the pack of male-dominated Nirvana followers because its liberating attitude calls for more than the same old party."

There were so many artists lumped into the angry-women genre—not just Hole, Babes in Toyland, and the Nymphs, but also 7 Year Bitch, L7, Lunachicks, Scrawl, Silverfish, Tribe 8, Burning Bush, Thrush, Queen Meanie Puss, Snatch, Pop Smear, Thrust, Spitboy, Ovarian Trolley, Dickless, and Polly Jean (PJ) Harvey—that all they really shared was a sense of righteous anger. They shied away from their angry-women label probably because it had been bestowed upon them—by men, no less—making their rage seem trivial and even a little clichéd. As in riot grrrl, they were all (or mostly) female rock bands playing loud, metallic rock juxtaposed with emotionally visceral imagery. The names of the songs and albums reverberated with a heady mixture of femininity and rage—Hole's album *Pretty on the Inside*, Babes in Toyland's "Bruise Violet," PJ Harvey's "Dry." In the venerable punk tradition of ironically naming yourself after phallic symbols and exaggerated masculinity (Revolting Cocks, Dickies, Meat Puppets, and Fishbone), these band names often included references to female stereotypes and anatomy (Hole, Ovarian Trolley, Snatch, and Burning Bush).

Mirroring the music, their favored style was the so-called kinderwhore look that included baby doll dresses, tiaras, Mary Janes, and smeared glittery makeup. It was virtually identical to riot grrrl style, perhaps a bit less juvenile and a bit more femme. It's worth noting that the look was a powerful one for boys as well—not to objectify, but to adopt as their own. Kurt Cobain, who was heterosexual, was frequently photographed wearing dresses and makeup. Joon Lee, a professor of English and gender studies at the Rhode Island School of Design who grew up in Iowa City, had to deal in the heartland of America not only with being a first-generation Asian immigrant but also with being gay. After a childhood spent listening to the opera *Carmen*, he discovered grunge. "Here was mainstream culture where boys could wear dresses and smeared lipstick and still project as boy. I could not go to school in a dress per se, but it was my version of the punk moment in the eighties. We could be outrageous and sexually strange and not get beat up every day."

Thurston Moore, a guitarist and lead singer in the band Sonic Youth and one of the most influential men in the independent music scene, coined the term "foxcore" to describe the angry-women phenomenon. "I remember hearing the term 'foxcore,'" says Lois Maffeo, "and thinking, Well, great, that puts down thousands of hours of work women have put into doing meetings and flyering and making fanzines. Thanks for reducing it to this completely shallow term." It's easy to see why Maffeo might bristle at the term, which seemed to fetishize these "rough" women, but

Moore likely didn't mean it to sound pejorative—he and Sonic Youth had long been supporters of women in music, offering opening slots at their shows to Babes in Toyland, Bikini Kill, and Hole. "I'm sure a part of Thurston was joking," says Megan Jasper of Sub Pop, the Seattle-based label perhaps best known as the spiritual home to grunge. "I don't know any women at the time who were offended. When you label anything like that, there's an implied eye roll."

Indie stalwarts could accuse these bands of being simply riot grrrl lite, but their brief ubiquity also succeeded in polishing the rough edges off what was seen by some as a waning, dogmatic movement and legitimized the angry-female perspective for the masses. Mainstream America embraced several foxcore bands, seeing them as sisters to their favorite grunge bands. Their goal was more rocking out than revolution. Girl bands' ability to rock was sometimes met with amazement, as members of 7 Year Bitch recount in the riot grrrl zine *Girl Germs*: "'We're helping open [male audience members'] minds,' says lead singer Selene Vigil. 'Like, "Oh wow, you're women and you can play!" But it's like, No shit!' Adds drummer Valerie Agnew, 'Just think about how many all-boy bands we sat through!'"

The outspokenness of these artists was nothing short of revelatory for some girls. "I remember how scared I was of men when I started college in 1991, having been fed a steady diet of rape-prevention strategies at my all-girls high school," says the foxcore fan Annie Frisbie. "The spate of TV movies about rape combined with the heavily publicized Take Back the Night rallies that were springing up everywhere to create a culture where I felt that the only way I could be safe was to armor myself with the girl power identity." So she sang along to Hole songs and went to classes with unwashed hair. "It wasn't about attracting men, but about saying things that had never been said before. They might have been girls, but they weren't children."

If riot grrrl was about emotional exhibitionism—making public via a zine or a song your own abuse or body issues—then the foxcore bands' exhibitionism was more corporeal. One legendary incident that has made it to the annals of many "most shocking rock moments" lists took place at the 1992 Reading Festival in England. L7's guitarist Donita Sparks, in response to mud being hurled at the band by the audience, flung a tampon into the audience with the scream "Eat my used tampon, assholes" (or, alternately, "fuckers"—accounts vary). The "tampon into audience" (or pantomime thereof) became a somewhat common trope. The writer and editor Holly Siegel grew up in the leafy and liberated neighborhood of Park Slope in Brooklyn, where Theo Kogan from the band Lunachicks was her occasional babysitter. She went to go see the band play at Coney Island High when she was fifteen. "I went backstage to see Theo, and had to pretend like the whole scene back there was normal to me." Even though Siegel fancied herself a badass city kid, she was far more virtuous and innocent than the teenage scenesters hanging around smoking and drinking. Needless to say, she felt a little awkward. Kogan was doing her makeup and asked Siegel if she could go get her a tampon. She dutifully bought one and brought it back to her. "She just took it out of the plastic and smashed the cotton into a pan of sparkly red lipstick. During the show, she pretended to pull it out, and holding it by the string, threw it lasso-style over her head and then into the audience," says Siegel. "I think I learned a feminist lesson that night." The foxcore bands were unafraid of a grand gesture—in this case, drawing attention to parts of the body that had previously been considered too shameful and certainly too feminine for rock.

While none of the foxcore bands achieved the fame of Nirvana, Pearl Jam, Soundgarden, or any number of other bands of the era, they did gain a ubiquity not in music but in marketing. Hole, Babes in Toyland, and L7 all had videos in heavy rotation on MTV and were signed to major labels, therefore reaching a success riot grrrl never achieved, or sought. The fact that they embraced major labels was a crucial distinction, and part of their success. Independent record companies (like K Records, Matador, Harriet, and Kill Rock Stars) had historically been friendly places for women musicians but offered relatively little, particularly in the pre-Internet, pre-digital-download era, in the way of distribution, recording technology, publicity, or money. The underground may have been an aesthetically purer place for women in music—there were no executives around trying to exert control over image, for example—but it was at the cost of financial security; few women artists were able to earn enough money off music to support a lifestyle beyond that of a college student, let alone provide for a family.

Accusations of selling out were lobbed about in the early part of the nineties so frequently that what exactly defined "selling out" became distinguishable only to the accuser. The eighties were a decade when the mainstream was inhospitable to the underground: Tipper Gore's Parents Music Resource Center attempted to pass laws regulating artistic expression, and ultimately succeeded at getting major labels to adopt parental advisory warning labels on albums; the Dead Kennedys' Jello Biafra was put on trial for obscenity; and some larger zines were having a hard time finding printers to even print them. Despite, or maybe because of, these reasons, the underground was fertile. The fan base of independently made music was growing and becoming sizable enough to warrant its own music conventions (South by Southwest), industry periodicals (*College Music Journal*), and monikers ("college rock").

In fact, the desire for worldly success was a kind of currency in the foxcore scene. Consider the Courtney Love–penned diatribe seeking a bass player for Hole, which is included in her published diary, *Dirty Blonde*: "Someone who can play ok, and stand in front of 30,000 people, take off her shirt and have fuck you written on her tits. If you're not afraid of me and you're not afraid to fucking say it, send a letter. No more pussies, No more fake girls, I want a whore from hell." The ideas of embracing pejorative words like "whore" and calling attention to the objectification of the body by scrawling across it were virtually identical to the tenets of riot grrrl, with one key difference: Love's ad invokes a stadium filled to capacity, not some all-ages club with a limit of a couple hundred; her ambition was plain from the outset.

Love quickly emerged as the breakout star of the foxcore musicians. After a peripatetic childhood living in the United States, New Zealand, and England, she had become a fixture on the outer rung of the West Coast indie-music scene. Her over-the-top persona and unapologetic will to power were so infamous that Lois Maffeo even had a short-lived band named after her. Love became much better known for her relationship with Kurt Cobain, whom she met at an L7 concert. The media's obsession with Kurtney, as they were called, came at a time in the early nineties when it was becoming increasingly easier to gather and disseminate celebrity pictures and news—and when the culture of celebrity worship was just beginning to coalesce. Love and

Babes in Toyland's Kat Bjelland, who were sometimes friends and sometimes bandmates, feuded over who had come up with the kinderwhore look that they both favored. In the early nineties, hard rock meant being dirty—the Seattle scene wasn't called "grunge" for nothing—and being unapologetically feminine was, if not shameful, then a little bit suspect. So seeking out fame was something else Love refused to apologize for, saying that she wanted to be a conventionally attractive star all along.

It is Love's relationship to beauty that makes her such a compelling figure. The first Hole album was called *Pretty on the Inside*. The title invites a dual interpretation: that beauty is projected from within, or alternatively, that, particularly for women, it no longer mattered what your insides felt like as long as your outside was in order. Love's early nineties zine was called *And She's Not Even Pretty*, and her devotion to the kinderwhore look was a way, sort of, to look pulled together and acceptably pretty, no matter how much rage and confusion she felt on the inside. As the writer Lisa Levy once said about Love, "Appearing in public with your messed-up insides showing—something Love frequently does—definitely gets noticed."

In Love's worldview, for women there's a dichotomy between the inside (what women think and feel) and the outside (appearance, that is, all that society seemed to care about) that can never be resolved. "When women get angry," she told Simon Reynolds in a 1992 article, "they are regarded as shrill or hysterical." She cites a mid-eighties all-girl hardcore band called Frightwig. "Because they were ugly, they were easy to dismiss as uptight feminists. One way around that, for me, is bleaching my hair and looking good. It's bad that I have to do that to get my anger accepted." She added with a self-conscious flourish that has become her trademark, "But then I'm part of an evolutionary process. I'm not the fully evolved end."

Love and the foxcore bands shared an anger that was subtly different than that of riot grrrl. The former's anger was expressed as appearing tough and gnarly, which was itself a feminist statement in the male-dominated hard-rock scene, while riot grrrl bands were generally angry at the status quo. By the mid-nineties, singers like Alanis Morissette, Meredith Brooks, and Fiona Apple had risen to fame as a further iteration of the angry woman in rock. They were angry, but so much more acceptable (read: pretty and unthreatening) than their predecessors, establishing themselves in the mainstream in ways that Hole or L7 never managed and riot grrrl would never dream of.

Morissette was a Canadian former child star who signed to Madonna's Maverick record label for her 1995 international debut album, *Jagged Little Pill*, and scored a hit with the first single, "You Oughta Know," which chronicled the demise of a love affair. Its lyrics, directed at an ex-lover (said to be the comedian Dave Coulier, best known as Uncle Joey on the sitcom *Full House*), were raw and, at times, graphic: "It was a slap in the face how quickly I was replaced/Are you thinking of me when you fuck her?"

Her music was undeniably pop, and the combination of edgy lyrics and a hummable chorus proved to be incredibly relatable. Sarah Wilson discovered her music as a teenager. "My friends and I would blast Alanis Morissette from my Volvo speakers as a stab at retaliation at the boys who dumped us, as we drove past their football practice after school." It was strange for some indie fans to see little girls blithely singing along to a song whose lyrics included references to going down on a guy in a theater. Melissa Laux, who spent her teen years obsessed with Siouxsie Sioux, the vocalist in the British group Siouxsie and the Banshees, accompanied her college boyfriend when he took his eleven-year-old sister and three of her friends to see Morissette play the Greek Theatre in Berkeley, California. "They were so excited by the energy, but obviously too young to really understand it. The concert tees have some 'men are bastards'–style statement on them and they wanted to buy them, which felt wrong."

For the journalist Evelyn McDonnell, who wrote about L7, PJ Harvey, Bikini Kill, and Tribe 8 in outlets like *Spin*, *Rolling Stone*, and *The New York Times* in the nineties, there was a shift in the country in the early part of the decade, when "for once the underground and mainstream matched instead of ran against each other." The trendiness of that music was also its downfall. "The music industry saw that riot grrrl was something people want," says McDonnell. But since they couldn't sign Bikini Kill or Bratmobile, they decided to "put out this angry psychotic Alanis record and create something called girl power."

And Morissette's influence was much more far-reaching than anything that had come out of Olympia. You didn't have to be culturally elite to discover her music, which was widely played on MTV and major radio stations. That kind of music, says Gayle Wald, "could be incredibly supportive for girls that discovered it. Riot grrrl was less accessible both aesthetically and in its production values." Morissette even told *The New York Times* that she wished that she had herself to listen to at fourteen, while suffering from an eating disorder and low self-esteem.

In his *New York Times* article on angry women of rock, Simon Reynolds quotes *Backlash* author Susan Faludi, who had said that "anger is not something that's an admirable trait in woman, whereas the angry young man is a hero." Music had long been an outlet for angry women; the nineties was about the normalization of female rage. Regardless of whether or not her music was the most authentic or the most innovative, Morissette's popularity went a long way toward creating a template for the acceptably angry woman in rock.

Soon, more solo angry-female rockers appeared. There was Meredith Brooks, whose song "Bitch" declared, "I'm a bitch/I'm a tease/I'm a goddess on my knees," seeking to redefine the insult as a sort of catch-all synonym for all that is womanly. Tracy Bonham's "Mother Mother" was sung from the perspective of a young woman out in the real world: "Mother mother can you hear me/ yeah I'm sober/sure I'm sane/Life is perfect/never better/still your daughter/still the same." Both were almost novelty songs, self-contained one-hit wonders that spoke to the prevailing fashion for independent women.

When her debut album, *Tidal*, went triple platinum in 1996, Fiona Apple, a singer and pianist, was the next to become an overnight success, due at least in part to her sexually and emotionally frank lyrics. In "Shadowboxer," she sings to an ex, "Once my lover, now my friend/What a cruel thing to pretend/What a cunning way to condescend." The album's biggest hit was "Criminal," a slutty masterpiece in which Apple sings of feeling like a criminal for being a "bad, bad girl" who needs to suffer for her sexual sins. In the accompanying video, she luxuriates on shag carpets and in hot tubs, smirking while singing about the sweet shame that can result from getting the pleasure that you want (but feel guilty for wanting in the first place). Apple's genius was that she knew how thrilling it feels to flaunt sexuality and she made it look, to my nineteen-year-old self, incredibly alluring. Even though she and I were the same age, Apple had spent her teen years gathering the kind of life experiences that allowed her to write lyrics about a girl "breaking a boy" just because she can. I, on the other hand, was a graduate of the self-defense class Model Mugging and had as a personal mantra "I'm scary not scared."

She was also beautiful (typically, *The New York Times* mentioned "the pouty bee-stung lips. The taut, pierced belly exposed by a flouncy shirt. The cascading honey-brown hair. And those eyes. Is this the next waif supermodel?"), preternaturally talented, and outspoken, which made her a favorite with the press.

One issue that the media brought up repeatedly was a rape in her early adolescence, a subject that the singer seemed to have a highly ambivalent attitude about discussing in public. She sang about it in "Sullen Girl": "They don't know I used to sail the deep and tranquil sea/But he washed me ashore and he took my pearl/And left an empty shell of me." An interview with *Rolling Stone* in 1998 suggests that if she "shares her problems, it is to normalize them, not to offer them up as public melodrama." But still, she told *The New York Times* in 1997, she didn't "want to be like the rape poster girl." She has no problem sharing her traumatic experience—which was surely important to countless fans—but she never makes any larger societal connection that takes any blame away from herself.

Bands like Bikini Kill saw rape as a larger societal problem. In "White Boy," a survivor of sexual assault sings, "I'm so sorry if I'm alienating some of you/Your whole fucking culture alienates me." And in "Liar," "Deny, you live your life in denial/Stand my whole life on trial." This new crop of angry female rockers like Morissette, Brooks, Bonham, and Apple may have had the ear of the mainstream media, but they lacked a community of their own; there were no consciousness-raising sessions or zines to pass around. Their music lacked the grassroots, organic component of networks and communities that indie music had always had as its trump card. The emphasis on the collective over the individual was a crucial distinction between real feminism and feminist-flavored rock.

One well-known artist who was able to connect her experiences to society at large was Tori Amos, who, like Apple, had also been an outspoken survivor of rape and played confessional, piano-based music. The song "Me and a Gun" on her 1991 breakthrough album, *Little Earthquakes*, was an a cappella first-person account of a rape and its aftermath. In 1994, she cofounded and became a spokesperson for the nonprofit Rape, Abuse and Incest National Network (RAINN), which connects callers with local rape crisis centers and has become a lobbying organization.

A similar instinct led Exene Cervenka, an LA punk pioneer in the band X, to cofound the Bohemian Women's Political Alliance, a collective of members who identified themselves as "the weird girls who didn't fit in. We are the little girls your parents wouldn't let you play with. We are the teenagers who dressed in black, the bad girls who climbed out of our bedroom windows after dark and caught taxis home at dawn. We are the daughters of Lilith, Lily Munster, Patti Smith and Emma Goldman." Their manifesta's demands included free health care and education, a redistribution of wealth, and "a reinstatement of the matriarchy." They didn't just dwell on the impossible, though. Their first action was to throw a tea party to benefit the Senate election campaign for the California politician Barbara Boxer (who won).

The Bohemian Women weren't alone. The same era brought Strong Women in Music, which was a New York–based group who wanted to discuss their role in the music community; musicians campaigning for abortion rights in Rock for Choice; and nineties indie bands like Superchunk and Mudhoney covering new wave songs for a compilation (very beloved to my teenage self and one of the first to herald eighties nostalgia) called *Freedom of Choice*, whose proceeds went to Planned Parenthood. Writing in *The New York Times*, Ann Powers said that this resurgence of political activism was important for providing "a space for women who have long played the role of 'one of the boys,' among musicians, artists, writers and other unconventional types, to discover their ties to other women."

Women whose sex appeal read more dominantly than their political discourse were met with some degree of suspicion from women like Cervenka, who had a more activist approach to her feminism. "I kind of call it 'Rod Stewart Feminism,'" she told *New York* magazine in 1996. "It's kind of the same mentality, which is if it's okay for guys to do it, it's okay for girls to do it. Tori Amos straddling a piano bench—is that empowering women or is that *Penthouse*-ing women? I don't know." But a dedication to honest sexual discourse and reclaiming their sexuality, which all these women were invested in, was inherently political. Whether it's the artist, the critics, or her audience who gets to decide if she's really in control of her sexuality was something all these women were working through. In the same article, the "One of Us" singer and avowed feminist Joan Osborne notes that an "ingredient of rock has always been this sexual display, and women have been more and more finding out a way that they can do that. Instead of being just a chick in the spandex with the teased-up hair that all the guys want to screw, it's more like, 'Yeah, this is how I'm going to project my sexuality, and these are my desires.'"

While most of the male rock bands that became hallmarks of nineties music—Pavement, Nirvana—shied away from displays of virility, women in rock were sexually assertive and proudly voracious. Perhaps no other artist of that era, male or female, did a better job of projecting her sexual desires than Liz Phair. She was considered an angry woman (albeit sultry-angry) when her first album, *Exile in Guyville*, said to be a track-for-track response to the Rolling Stones' *Exile on Main Street*, came out in 1993. She wasn't an especially talented vocalist or guitar player, but she was blond, clean-cut, and possessed a liberal arts education from the Chicago suburbs. The dirtiness of her lyrics captivated her critics. "Every time I see your face/I get all wet between my legs" she sang in "Flower." In "Glory" it was "He's got a really big tongue." "Shatter" dealt with the conscience of the sexually voracious female: "I know that I don't always realize/How sleazy it is/messing with these guys." *Sassy* magazine's review of *Exile* gushes that "orgasmic is not too strong a word to use here." As Phair told *Elle* upon the release of the fifteenth anniversary reissue of *Exile*, "People thought it was this straight-up confessional diary of this naive person. I thought, 'Don't you get it's kind of funny and I kind of know what I'm doing?'" Women loved that Phair occupied such a male space—that she was the objectifier, in control of her own desire, and ready to act on it.

"I knew why every male journalist wanted to write about her and wanted to go see her," Marcelle Karp, one of the cofounders of *Bust* magazine, says with a laugh. "Because they were thinking about her giving them blow jobs." But her sexual frankness was also threatening. "I heard a lot of men saying that they were listening to my album because someone told them they should,"

Phair told *New York*. "Then one day they suddenly heard the words and it flipped them out. They all expressed this powerful feeling of being both fired at and caught, like, for being what they are. And the women were like, 'Well, I heard the words from the beginning, and they made perfect sense to me.'" It was rare for a woman to sing from that point of view, and Phair's greatest champions were her young female fans. The album became an instant classic, a nineties version of Joni Mitchell's *Blue* or Stevie Nicks's *Bella Donna* or other albums that captured the emotional tenor of largely white, middle-class women. Listening to *Exile*, a woman is able to feel just like she did at eighteen (or fifteen or however old she was when she discovered Phair), lying on the floor of her dorm room, enraptured by the level of truth being spoken, amazed that someone out there gets the complications of her existence.

Phair balked at being a poster girl for third wave feminism. "I don't want to be anyone's revolutionary," she told *New York*. "I don't want to lead a movement. I mean, it turns me off so much. I never saw music as a way—and a lot of people do, especially riot grrrls—to make change happen. I never, ever saw it that way. I still don't. Anyone with any kind of sensitivity beyond their general age group knows you can't tidy life up like that." Whatever her fans' vision of the direction her career should go in, she embarked on what would be an untidy life. After *Exile*'s critical accolades and her appearance as one of the very few women to land a solo cover of *Rolling Stone*, she married her boyfriend, had a child, and produced albums that disappointed many among her cult following. By the end of the nineties, she had jumped ship from Matador, the indie label that had championed her early career, to Capitol Records, where she transformed herself into a pop star: moving to Los Angeles, writing songs with the hit-making production team the Matrix, releasing her fourth album with a blandly eponymous title, and actively courting the middlebrow. Her persona remained sexy—she was photographed wearing miniskirts and posing suggestively with her guitar—but it had a compulsory gloss to it. Gone was the young woman who had taken sexuality in her own hands and spoken of it with the bravado of Mick Jagger, and in her place was something a little more Stepford: a singer who had a sexy image because a blond, conventionally attractive woman wearing tall boots sold more records.

The persona might have changed, but the sex remained—Phair's eponymous fourth album included a song called "H.W.C." for "hot white cum." Phair's attempts to transform herself into mainstream sexy were only somewhat successful. Even though she scored the biggest hit of her career in 2003 with the single "Why Can't I?" which was used on movie and television sound tracks, her core fans found her bid to be a young, sexy pop star embarrassing and she became a too-easy joke, never achieving the level of stardom she was after. In interviews, Phair has maintained that she had always wanted to be a mainstream artist, and it would be patronizing to doubt her stated intentions. After all, so much of her appeal has come from her inability to be anything but herself. At the same time, it's vastly disappointing to think that the singer who deadpanned, "I want to be your blow job queen" had always secretly aspired to a more mundane existence.

If Phair claimed she always craved mainstream acceptance and lacked any internal struggle with feminist values, then Courtney Love is her opposite. Love always wants to reassure the public that she's still punk rock, that she's still a feminist, that she's still authentic and legitimate, no matter how much cosmetic surgery she appears to have had or how much weight she's shed. By the time she married Cobain, she was rumored to have undergone rhinoplasty and to have had breast implants. But it was her brief late-nineties makeover into a bobbed, Versace-wearing fashion icon (which coincided with critical acclaim playing a stripper in her role in *The People vs. Larry Flynt*) that was most memorable for launching her acceptance into the Hollywood and fashion community. Love always couched her glam makeover in feminist rhetoric, as if she were doing it to support herself, and purely as a means to get her ideas heard by as many people as possible. Even her most ardent fans must have had difficulty accepting, in the summer of 2007, her newly emaciated body, rumored to be a result of bariatric surgery or liposuction (or just, as Love claimed, a diet of energy shakes, fish, and vegetables). At a concert in Manhattan in July 2007, she asked the crowd to excuse her while she chugged a protein drink between songs, saying she "had to take care of my eating disorder." Of course, she then said she was joking and added, "I don't have an eating disorder." Love is the mess we all are inside, struggling with feminist ideals while flirting with the overwhelming tug of mainstream values. Even when she contradicts herself, you know at that moment she's speaking her truth.

Yet despite her film roles, modeling, or straightforward rock albums (like Hole's final album, *Celebrity Skin*), the "normal" American public is never going to accept Love. At the same time, she has become anathema to indie fans after she abandoned the punk community for Hollywood (literally moving from Seattle to Beverly Hills). Instead, Love, whom *Rolling Stone* called "the most controversial woman in the history of rock," has become infamous for her many alleged transgressions: being a stripper, being ambitious, and, most of all, being a bad widow. After flirting equally with riot grrrl and the mainstream and failing to find a place where she fit, she now occupies our collective consciousness— often unfairly—as a polarizing figure and a tabloid favorite, Yoko Ono but more dangerous.

Female artists are so objectified that they almost can't exist without a mid-career makeover. Juliana Hatfield, the daughter of a Boston fashion editor, wrote mildly pissed off songs that mirrored high school diary entries (with lyrics like "Now, here comes the song I love so much/Makes me wanna go fuck shit up/Now, I got Nirvana in my head/I'm so glad I'm not dead") and became in the early nineties a sort of pinup icon for disaffected teen girls. Her videos frequently appeared on MTV and she was photographed for the cover of *Sassy* brandishing a guitar. (The fact that, in her mid-twenties, she admitted in an interview to being a virgin probably helped her relatability factor to a teen demographic.) In her nineties heyday, she wore dark eyeliner, had short, dyed hair, and dressed like a tomboy. Her music remained more or less the same, but ten years later she was playing shows at the Bowery Ballroom in New York with expensively highlighted hair à la Jennifer Aniston. I went, expecting to see the venue packed with other girls in their late twenties who wanted to relive their angsty teen years. Instead, it was filled with lecherous guys who kept yelling about how hot she was. Soon after her memoir came out in 2008, she checked into a clinic to treat an eating disorder she had been dealing with since adolescence. She blogged about the experience for fans.

It's all enough to make Alanis Morissette seem like a welcome exception. Morissette also had a teenage eating disorder, subsisting on black coffee to drop weight to please her record company.

But a decade after *Jagged Little Pill*'s release, her body had grown more womanly than in her early twenties. Yet she's still no icon of body acceptance—in 2008, she told tabloids how much she loved the way she looked, then lost twenty pounds on a vegan diet and gave a new round of interviews that same year, complete with photos of her posing in vinyl leggings, about how much better she felt.

There was at least one popular female artist whose message was less mixed. Ani DiFranco, or Ani, as she is universally known to her fans, was, to a certain kind of white, middle-class woman, girl power in the purest sense. At twenty, she founded her own record label, Righteous Babe. She's released dozens of albums (and has sold over four million copies), had a baby, documented her life on the road, and opened for Bob Dylan. (Andi Zeisler went to go see DiFranco open for Bob Dylan at Foxwoods Casino in Connecticut. "Ani stopped singing and chastised the girls in the audience for singing so loudly that Ani was having trouble hearing herself," she remembers. "You could tell she felt bad, but at the same time, I could detect a sense in her that it had gotten out of control. And then when Bob Dylan came on, these girls booed because they wanted more Ani. I wonder if she gets sick of it?") She even had a sense of humor. When her fan Fiona Garlich saw her play at Oregon State University, DiFranco made a sly comment about the mascot being the beaver and "everyone cheered." An avowed feminist activist and an outspoken bisexual, DiFranco has been candid about the necessity of women musicians identifying with the F-word. "Either you are a feminist or you are a sexist/misogynist," she once wrote. "There is no box marked 'other.'" She specializes in purposeful lyrics like "I am a poster girl with no poster/I am thirty-two flavors and then some/

and I'm beyond your peripheral vision/so you might want to turn your head/cause someday you're going to get hungry/and eat most of the words you just said."

Although all these disparate bands and solo artists were collectively considered "angry women," they weren't part of any overarching movement. There was no platform, no takeaway. If a girl got inspired from seeing Alanis Morissette or Liz Phair, then what? The musicians and fans needed a rallying point, and Lilith Fair was created to fill the void.

Despite what seemed like significant commercial and critical strides, when Sarah McLachlan tried to book a tour with her fellow singer-songwriter Paula Cole, promoters told her that no one would come to see two women on the same bill. So she started Lilith Fair, a festival of music made by women that toured the United States and Canada from 1997 to 1999. It was a time when there were few women playing at the traveling alterna-fest Lollapalooza, and the supermacho Ozzfest, H.O.R.D.E., and Warped tours were taking in millions a year in ticket sales, marketing themselves to teenage boys. The 1999 Woodstock anniversary concert, which featured performances by the Red Hot Chili Peppers and Limp Bizkit, both a far cry from the peacenik bands of the 1969 version, was marred by reports of several rapes, with at least one gang rape allegedly taking place in the mosh pit, near the front of the stage. If music festivals were going to be such inhospitable places for women (both as band members and fans), Lilith was a refreshing alternative.

To prove her gender's commercial viability, McLachlan booked Lilith with a roster of rock chicks (Liz Phair, Juliana Hatfield, the Indigo Girls, the Dixie Chicks) and confessional singer-songwriters (Fiona Apple, Shawn Colvin, Paula Cole, Lisa Loeb,

Beth Orton, Jewel, Suzanne Vega). The 1997 Lilith Fair tour took in $16 million, making it that year's highest-grossing touring festival. In addition to enjoying the music, audience members could use the festival as an opportunity for activism through its emphasis on feminist charities (one dollar from each ticket sold benefited a local women's organization) and activity booths.

Perhaps most important, it enacted one of the hallmarks of feminism by creating one of the few women-centric spaces for the mainstream. Radicals, riot grrrls, and women from various subcultures had access to such separatist women-only spaces, and had benefited from the experience of life without men, whether that meant speaking more freely, carrying oneself differently, feeling a sense of safety, or escaping sexual commodification. Most women rarely got these opportunities, and McLachlan offered them a version of collective feminist activity that was missing from mainstream music.

For some, the festival signified feminist freedom. Fiona Garlich attended the first year of the tour and remembers it feeling "really significant" to her college-age self. She had spent her high school years listening to classical music (her idea of current was the Beatles), so female singer-songwriters like Dar Williams and Tracy Chapman were an entry into feminism. "Hearing music sung in a strong female voice was inspirational back then, as my own identity was just starting to take form. I think it represented a time in my life when I was awakening to the world and started to think of myself as a woman. I also started to feel an affinity for women as a group, an oppressed group that needed fighting for." She jokes that she let her leg and armpit hair grow long, "both out of laziness and as a statement against the patriarchy."

I never attended a Lilith Fair—the music seemed too self-consciously feminine, the sense of community contrived. A writer in *Salon* dismissed the Lilith aesthetic for its hippieish "Massengil–meets–Celestial Seasonings vibe," which sums up the sentiment that a lot of women felt. "Lilith didn't speak to my version of being a woman," says Bernie Bankrupt from the band Lesbians on Ecstasy. Sheri Hood likens the scene to a guilty pleasure: "Lilith bands are the musical equivalent of chick flicks. You might indulge in it, but it's not really where you want to be." Lilith was too broad and too homogenous for women who considered themselves serious music fans, but the target audience was much more mainstream than that, anyway. The real problem was that, rather than coming out of third wave feminist ideas, Lilith was a direct descendant of women's music, a genre that included singers like Holly Near or Cris Williamson, known for being earnest and folksy, and was more closely aligned to the ethos of second wave feminism than more current feminist ideas or musical stylings.

"It made me crazy when women were anti-Lilith," counters Carla DeSantis. "It didn't have to represent all women." DeSantis, who had a booth hawking copies of her magazine *Rockrgrl* on the West Coast dates, points out that there was some measure of diversity in the lineup, both in race and sound, particularly in the later years—Missy Elliott, Garbage, Erykah Badu. But the attempt at mixing musical genres meant that the tour itself had a less friendly feel. As time went on, there were fewer all-girl jam sessions or artists coming out and sitting in on one another's songs than in the first year, perhaps because of an increasingly corporate structure. A more diverse lineup made Lilith's latter years feel a little less clannish, but it also meant that all the artists weren't already acquainted and the ones who met while on tour didn't necessarily relate to women's music, or one another. "They didn't do a good job integrating because Missy Elliott was like, 'I'm coming with my crew. But we actually don't want to hang out with you,'" remembers Jennifer Baumgardner, who was dating the Indigo Girl Amy Ray at the time and traveling along with her. "Because it was more successful, they had to be more self-conscious." In terms of activism, Ray considers the three years she spent touring with Lilith an unqualified success because the tour donated money each night to a representative of a different worthy cause. "It got down to a grassroots level in a way that was pretty amazing. We presented the check at a press conference. We'd have a check, hand it to a woman, and she'd start crying. And it happened every night."

Lilith was a far less radical version of the long-running Michigan Womyn's Music Festival, ground zero for women's music in America. (It might have been a direct inspiration for Lilith—McLachlan has played there.) Since its founding in 1976, the festival has held a reputation, depending on to whom you're talking, as either the most nurturing or most divisive place on earth for women. It began as a folk festival put together by a group of ardently working-class Midwestern women and has grown to an annual festival entirely built by, staffed by, and made up of around four thousand women who convene on a remote location in western Michigan for a week of matriarchy during the full moon of each August. Everyone who attends must work a shift ranging from food preparation to driving shuttle buses, all musicians are paid the same amount, and there are workshops like "The Matrix of Oppression" and "Articulating Trauma." It is, as Amy Ray, both a repeat attendee and headliner, said, "so completely different from what happens in the world."

I had first learned about the festival from someone in college and had always been curious about going. I couldn't tell if the experience would be life-changing or traumatic. I knew that in researching this book, I had the opportunity to finally make the trip out there, so in August 2007, I went with two friends. I can say with complete certainty that the days that I spent at Michigan (or as we came to jokingly call it, "Mychygyn") were some of the strangest of my life. At first, I felt jaded. The festival felt like an odd but endearing relic of seventies feminism. Everywhere there were reminders of sisterhood and safety. There were signs that asked us to "please wear underwear" in the food lines. There were butch parades and femme parades and parades of redheads ("We are the redheads, the mighty, mighty redheads, everywhere we go, people want to know who we are, so we tell them . . ."). It was a matriarchy, and apparently matriarchy meant never having to look or wait for a toilet, because there were porta-johns (called by all, naturally, porta-janes) everywhere—spotless, fully stocked with toilet paper, and with hand sanitizer, to boot. At the crafts bazaar, I saw a gold dildo in the shape of a sperm whale, many batik sarongs, multiple T-shirts celebrating the divine within, a device that allows you to pee while standing, buttons with photos of Joan Jett and Jane Fonda, and myriad images of Celtic knots, wolves, and moons. I saw a CD with song titles that included "Dark Chocolate," "When Cats Rule the World," and (my favorite) "Menstrual Tango." All food was accompanied by the holy trinity of condiments from my college years: tamari, Tabasco sauce, and brewer's yeast. All three signified healthy food that needs to be mildly spiced up, which felt symbolic of the festival's aesthetic.

The music was the part I was least looking forward to. I've been a fan of music by women my whole life, but women's music always felt like something that belonged to my mother's generation. I was more than happy to deride and write off an entire genre that I felt hinged on the assumption that women wanted to hear nurturing, earnest music. I can't say that I loved the music at the festival, but it wasn't all acoustic folk songs, as I had feared. I heard covers of Queen and the Bee Gees and Led Zeppelin and a version of Khia's 2002 song "My Neck, My Back," whose oft-repeated chorus of "My neck, my back, lick my pussy and my crack" was a sing-along hit with both the older Midwestern attendees and the younger crowd. Music didn't always feel like the focal point; or, I should say, the die-hard older women seemed to come to Michigan for the performances but the younger generation seemed to be there to frolic in the woods. Sometimes I think I heard more sex noises coming from tents than music from the stage.

Over the years, the organizers have tried to inject some new blood into the festival. Kathleen Hanna's band Le Tigre has played, and the year I attended, two young feminist punk bands, Lesbians on Ecstasy and Erase Errata, performed. Evelyn Mc-Donnell traveled there in 1994, the first year that the San Francisco queercore band Tribe 8 appeared at the festival. "It was the old guard versus the new guard." There were protests. "I was at this festival that was every horrible cliché of women's music. It was totally not hip," she says. And yet, "it is really amazing to be in a place with only women. I felt like there was a way in which I had lost my self-consciousness and objectification. It was an enlightening and powerful feeling."

Rosemary, my shift leader at a work session, was the one person I encountered who most underscored why a festival like this was necessary. While I was busy trying not to smirk at the drum circles and the songs about cats, here was a sixty-something butch grandma of ten from Normal, Illinois, who got one week a year to experience feminist separatist bliss. The festival was just as vital for her as Lilith Fair was for some women or Heavens to Betsy concerts had been to me. (She also gave a much-needed reminder that even amid all women, there are still sexual predators, saying that if anything happened to us, to go to the S&M camp "because those girls will take care of you.")

The Michigan festival is a microcosm of all the debates that happen within feminism—the internal struggles about what the movement should and shouldn't represent, what it should look like and sound like, if it needs to grow. Whether that growth should include transgendered women has become the festival's hot-button issue. The organizer Lisa Vogel's strongly held "womyn-born-womyn" policy—which admits to the festival those born with female genitalia only—meant that trans women weren't welcome. In fact, only boys under the age of six are allowed on festival grounds (with the exception of the male workers who come each night to empty the porta-janes, followed by a volunteer chanting, "Man on the land," to notify everyone of their presence), and even they are sequestered in the Brother Sun camp near the massive parking lots.

After a trans woman, Nancy Burkholder, was kicked out of the Michigan Womyn's Music Festival in 1991 when she revealed her transsexual status, another festival, Camp Trans, was created a few years later as both a protest and an alternative. For a certain kind of open-minded third wave feminist, no visit to Michigan would be complete without going to Camp Trans, which skews younger, hipper, and dirtier than the Womyn's festival.

I wanted to visit Camp Trans, but it was awkward going from the huge, beautiful private land to a dusty campsite a quarter mile down the road, feeling like a sexual tourist. We arrived just in time for the daily "community meeting" where a group of trans people and their friends sat in a very large circle. Everyone said their name and preferred pronoun. I said, "My name is Marisa, I prefer female pronouns, I'm visiting from the other festival," and I'm not sure if I've ever been cheered so hard in my life. Just for showing up!

Camp Trans began in 1994, in the wake of the galvanizing energy of riot grrrl, and even though I didn't get to visit until over a decade later, it still had a righteous sense of indignation, more so than any of the so-called angry women of nineties rock ever had. It feels like a rightful heir to the boosterism and revolution riot grrrl promised with none of the cliquishness. Camp Trans had groups like "Team Friendly" (to greet visitors) and "Team Smoke You Out" (to get everyone stoned). It felt like the average age was about twenty-two, and it lacked the organization of the other festival, whose average age skewed more Baby Boomer. People at the community meeting would make announcements like, "Um, I need a ride to the airport? By eleven tomorrow morning? Or I'm going to get fired from my job?" or "Last night I had a water bottle and shoes and now I don't. Did anyone find them in the woods?" We watched performers much more homegrown than the national (albeit not necessarily chart-topping) acts that played for the womyn down the road: there was a skit based on group therapy, a lightbulb eater, and a song called "Mass Grave" that was the most purely punk music I had perhaps ever experienced. It was one of the friendliest and most accepting places I've been to in my life, where everyone wanted to chat and no one minded that I was a woman-born-woman from the other festival. And there is plenty of common ground. Both festivals have, as their primary goal, to allow women to connect with one another, which is certainly at the core of girl power. They reflect a more manageable movement, something that happens for just a week every summer that creates lasting bonds and inspires people for the rest of the year.

Camp Trans was an environment that, by virtue of generation, was one that was more familiar to me. While I appreciated the militancy of the Michigan Womyn's Music Festival, its exclusivity felt like a relic of the second wave, while Camp Trans felt more vital and its more flexible view of gender more centered in the future of feminist discourse. It was at once the purest, most raw and honest, and most unlikely expression of girl (or whatever gender you may choose) power that I have ever, or will ever, experience. I wasn't even there for the traditional full week—just a long weekend—and yet afterward it felt like I had to adjust to life back in the patriarchy. "I feel dazed. It was great and hard to describe and often really aesthetically awful, but also totally amazing," I wrote after I got home, in an e-mail to a friend accompanied by a photo of myself sitting next to a hand-painted sign for a trail called Labia Lane. "I'm glad I went."

sassy retort that they were "washing their hair" whenever the boys in school would ask them out. More punk than pop, the two collaborated on a fanzine for the indie band the Manic Street Preachers and released a few independent singles.

The artwork for their first album, 1993's *We Are Shampoo*, was simply a collage of Barbie dolls and candy wrappers. That celebration of the frivolity of life as a girl continued into their self-professed love for everything kitschy and plastic and pink and shiny. By 1994, their song "Trouble" was climbing the charts, and they appeared on *Top of the Pops* and the cover of *Smash Hits* (both milestones of mainstream British success). They had a song on the soundtrack to *Mighty Morphin Power Rangers: The Movie* and became hugely famous in Japan.

The Shampoo fan Miriam Bale had embraced riot grrrl as a teenager growing up in northern California but, by the mid-nineties, had begun to feel tired of its confrontational nature. "I was jaded from riot grrrl, but I still really believed in being a girl, so Shampoo really resonated," she says. "They had this line, 'Hippie chicks are sad/and supermodels suck/riot grrrls, diet girls, who really gives a fuck,' that really summed up my feelings at the time. They had a political edge, though—they were about their girl friendships being the most important thing and their male friendships were secondary to that." Julia Downes, a British veteran of riot grrrl, saw the band perform at an event at a clothing store in the United Kingdom when she was twelve, tagging along with her sister and mother. "It sounds stupid, but that definitely changed my life," she says. "I'd never seen anything like them before. They were rude, over the top, and my mum hated them. They just burst out and I was like, 'That's it, I'm going to change my whole outlook, sack off the politeness of playing violin and

3.

GIRL GROUPS

The 2001 edition of the *Oxford English Dictionary*, that éminence grise of the English language, included the phrase "riot grrrl," which was given the rather bare-bones definition of "a movement expressing feminist resistance to male domination in society." Another phrase added that year was "girl power," which was described as "a self-reliant attitude among girls and young women manifested in ambition, assertiveness and individualism." The distillation of the riot grrrl slogan "revolution girl-style now" into something more mainstream and palatable, girl power was, disturbingly, feminism without the activism—and it was a resounding success.

We have the Spice Girls to thank for the world domination of the catchphrase, but before they achieved cultural ubiquity, there was another, lesser-known British female pop group that championed girl power: Shampoo. Shampoo was made up of high school friends Jacqui Blake and Carrie Askew, who, if legend is to be believed, got the nickname "the shampoo girls" due to their singing in the choir, and get an electric guitar for my birthday and start a nasty trashy band.'"

Shampoo's wink-wink, arch take on girl power may not have been obvious enough for mass audiences. Their next album, in 1996, was called *Girl Power*, though by then many of their fans had moved on and they were considered a bit of a one-hit wonder. But another group was waiting in the wings to replace them.

The Spice Girls' beginnings were slightly inauspicious. In March 1994, hundreds of girls responded to an ad placed in Britain's *The Stage* newspaper asking: "R U 18–23 with the ability to sing/dance? R U streetwise, ambitious, outgoing and determined?" The ad was placed by Chris and Bob Herbert, a father-son management duo who were looking to manufacture a girl group that could compete with Britain's successful boy bands, like Take That. Five women made the cut to eventually become the Spice Girls: Victoria Adams (now Beckham) aka "Posh Spice," Emma Bunton aka "Baby Spice," Melanie Brown aka "Scary Spice," Melanie Chisholm aka "Sporty Spice," and Geri Halliwell aka "Ginger Spice."

Their platform was a nebulous pro-female concept called girl power, which included slogans such as "G-Force with a Zoom!" and "Silence Is Golden but Shouting Is Fun." Their lyrics and manifestas pushed sisterhood ("You stick with your mates and they stick with you") and equal rights ("I expect an equal relationship where he does as much washing up as I do").

So what exactly was the Spice Girls' definition of girl power? "Girl Power is about being able to do things just as well as the boys—if not better—and being who you wannabe," said Sporty. "Girl power is about equality and having fun and trying to rule your life," Scary told *New York*. In *Entertainment Weekly*, Baby was quoted as saying that "just because you've got a short skirt and a pair of tits, you can still say what you want to say. We're still very strong." "We're more than a band," Sporty told MTV, "we're a philosophy." The Spice Girls' official book, *Girl Power!*, declares "Girl Power is when . . . you believe in yourself and control your own life." While their message of girl power can be credited with giving feminism a sparkly sheen, they were also completely without political consciousness. Whether this brand of warmed-over feminism was their own idea or something constructed by their handlers we'll probably never know—the Spices were never off-message when it came to their signature slogan—but based on the enthusiasm with which they preached it, it's safe to say they were operating of their own accord. In 1996, Miriam Bale had just moved back to California after a few years spent living in London after high school. Her ex-boyfriend sent her the first Spice Girls album as a care package. "His note said that anyone who liked Shampoo would love the Spices, but it left me a little cold. There was no vitality or urgency to their music."

Their first hit, cowritten with two male songwriters, was 1996's "Wannabe," a bubblegum anthem to girl friendship impossible to get out of your head. It was sung by a bunch of girls who definitely looked like they would privilege romantic love with a guy over female friendship, but the lyrics, which addressed a prospective paramour, claimed otherwise. "If you wanna be my lover/ you gotta get with my friends/make it last forever/friendship never ends."

They certainly weren't the first pop singers to use the façade of feminism. In *The New York Times Magazine*, Deborah Solomon called Cyndi Lauper's 1983 hit "Girls Just Want to Have Fun" "the first feminist backlash song." "It came out in the 80s and goes against the preachy and high-minded tone of 70s feminism," Solomon says. Lauper protests in the article: "It's totally feminist. It's a song about entitlement. Why can't women have fun?" Originally, though, the song was written and sung by a man; Lauper refused to sing it because she thought it was anti-female. But after tweaking the lyrics herself, she agreed to record it. In the new version, Lauper sympathizes with her mother ("we're not the fortunate ones") and mocks her overbearing father ("daddy dear you know you're still number one"), both of whom are unhappy with her staying out all night.

The song, like "Wannabe," is a classic girl-power anthem that places girls in the middle of the song, interrogating the very condition of girlishness and celebrating what it is to be a girl or what it could be to be a girl. Girl-power anthems are written off as contrived and suitable only for the not-at-all-discerning tastes of teenage girls. Thirty years old when the song came out, Lauper was playacting at being a girl—and the ultimate girl, at that—with her Betty Boop voice and crazy dress-up outfits. Yet she managed to embody girl power by embracing the very third wave idea that being a girl, a girl who just wants to have fun, wasn't something to be denigrated. Lauper's song went where Betty Friedan—who hated frivolity—did not. The young girls who heard the song and saw the video could identify with Lauper dancing through the streets, rebelling against her father, commiserating with her mother, having a pillow fight with friends. And as girls who just wanted to have fun—and yet didn't *just* want to have fun—her fans were in on her joke.

The singer Mirah Zeitlyn has a photo of herself at age nine posing with great pride as she holds a copy of Lauper's *She's So Unusual*, which she had gotten for Christmas. It reminds her of a turning point in her own childhood. "You haven't quite discovered the world yet. It consists of your immediate surroundings and your little family unit. I feel like my concept of the broadness of the world around me happened then." She wasn't the only real-life girl who loved it. The music fan Karen Hester's first tape ever purchased was by Cyndi Lauper. Her mom even helped her dye her hair purple in homage to the singer's own streaked hair. Rachel Pine, another Lauper admirer, thinks, in retrospect, that she was the most empowering singer of the era because "she wasn't model-gorgeous like Belinda Carlisle, or tough like Joan Jett, nor did she possess the pipes of Pat Benatar, but because she was willing to go out and be herself, and be wacky, and wear a vintage dress and an army jacket with Chuck Taylor high-tops—so could I. Cyndi let everyone be who they were, or try being someone new—which is so crucially important when you're a teenage girl." Amanda Palmer, the singer for the Dresden Dolls, praised Lauper in a press release announcing that they were touring together. "Cyndi was one of my three main formative idols. I kid you not, I spent several hundred hours of my after-school life working on my choreography to the entire *She's So Unusual* record in my parents' living room. As to the holy trinity postered above my bed, I wanted to fuck Prince, I wanted to pose like Madonna . . . but I wanted to be Cyndi Lauper."

As a kid in the eighties, I sang along with Lauper (and years later figured out that my favorite song, "She Bop," was about masturbation), but Madonna was really my entry into girl power. I have a distinct memory of sitting on our kitchen counter and telling my mother how superior life seemed as a girl, my justification being that my gender could wear both pants and skirts. I was, after all, the only third-grader at Branciforte Elementary School circa 1985 who would regularly dress in full-on Madonna Boy Toy mode: a black glittery bow on my head, a shoulder-baring top. My most cherished object was a black coral cross, which I wore as an earring in one ear.

It's now difficult to even remember a time when Cyndi Lauper and Madonna were pitted against each other, dueling for the admiration of girls. But Madonna's will to power far and away exceeded Lauper's and, prior to the Spices, she was the dominant pop template. The singer was a jumble of contradictions: a working-class Catholic girl from Michigan whose job prior to her first hit was at a New York City donut shop. She dressed with a nod to punk (she's been accused of stealing early inspiration from both Viv Albertine of the Slits and Blondie's Debbie Harry) but desired fame above all else. She sold a vision of female independence, yet her two biggest hits of the era, "Material Girl" and "Like a Virgin," were both written by men—which was hardly a secret; Madonna was candid about her working relationships with male producers.

Eighties pop divas like Lauper and Madonna gave girls who weren't old enough, cool enough, or urban enough to dig deeper into the counterculture a fantasy of liberation—which would hopefully turn into real independence—that would be echoed again and again by pop singers around the world.

By the Spice Girls' inception in the mid-nineties, girls had been brought to the foreground, be it in bestselling books like Mary Pipher's *Reviving Ophelia* or in the American Association of University Women's report "How Schools Shortchange Girls," which landed on the front pages of many newspapers. As the so-called Generation Y or millennials (a population of approximately sixty million born between 1978 and '94, about three times the size of Gen X) came of age, a slew of pop culture creations geared toward teenagers appeared. Teen girl audiences emerged as one of the most powerful demographics of the era, making movies like *Clueless*, *Scream*, and *Titanic* massive hits. On television, more programming than ever began featuring sassy teen girl protagonists in shows like *Felicity*, *Dawson's Creek*, and *Buffy the Vampire Slayer*. The teen magazine market in the United States, which had previously maintained two or three titles, mushroomed. A new generation of junior versions of adult magazines—*Teen People*, *ELLEgirl*, *Teen Vogue*, and *CosmoGIRL!*—joined stalwarts like *Seventeen*, *YM*, and *Teen*. Artists, pop culture writers, and academics alike had taken to the idea of girl culture, in which the very essence of constructed notions of girlishness—shopping, dressing up, and yes, singing along to saccharine-sounding pop songs—was acknowledged as being both vital and important.

The Spice fan Hilary Davis was in elementary school when the Spices became popular. Girl power was something that she identified with. "I think that's why lots of girls liked them," she says. "It wasn't women power, and it wasn't female power, it was girl power." For her birthday one year—notable for being her first sleepover party—two different people gave her the movie *Spice World*. After she and her friends watched the movie, they partnered up and picked a Spice song to dance to. "Most girls wanted to be the Spice Girls, or wanted to be a single Spice Girl. It was a way to identify yourself, and make you feel like you had your own identity—I mean, back then we thought we had our own," she remembers. "It was a way to make you feel cool, like you were a part of something."

Of course, not every young girl carved her identity through them. The Period Pains, an all-girl teen band from England, released a single in the height of Spice mania in 1997 called "Spice

Girls (Who Do You Think You Are?)" with anti-Spice lyrics like "You can't even sing/wear bikinis on stage . . . you're not girls you're women/you're boring and you're lame." The musician and writer Claire Evans, who spent most of her teen years in Portland, Oregon, working on her website, the band Weezer's second-largest fan site, did not worship at the Spice altar. "It seemed like a new societal standard I wasn't a part of. They were girly and sexy and intimidating."

One of the keys to the success of the Spice Girls was that it was easy for girls to imagine being one of them. It didn't matter that the five women weren't particularly talented singers or dancers; it was their appearance of ordinariness—along with their message of total empowerment—that was their greatest asset. They were indeed styled and slick and beautiful, but not in a supermodel way, and as singers and dancers they were in possession of the kind of talent attainable to anyone with enough training and dedication—you didn't get a sense they would stand a chance on *American Idol.*

Their nicknames made them seem more like cartoon characters or superheroes, and broadened their appeal to various kinds of girls. "Now that I have a daughter, I really notice that these archetypes begin in the playground—in preschool, even," notes the *Bust* cofounder Marcelle Karp. "There is the girl who is a tomboy. There is a girl who's the sweet one. There's the one who's the loudmouth, and then there is the bully." Whether the Spice personae were a nefarious attempt to box up multifaceted women or just easily relatable shorthand for their young audience, they were, at the least, very memorable.

Each moniker was also a stereotype that could be seen as a product of the male gaze. In fact, one of the names was initially blunter: Halliwell began as "Sexy Spice," but she insisted that she found the name derogatory and asked to be referred to instead as "Ginger Spice," though I'd venture a guess that the name change was ultimately facilitated more by mass marketability and less by feminist ethos. At the same time, there was a homoerotic edge to their music, which the group coyly flirted with. When Scary underwent the particularly nineties ritual of getting her tongue pierced, she supposedly made her fellow Spices kiss her to see how it felt. Ginger sometimes commented on the breasts of fellow celebrities, and the group not only embraced their lesbian fans, but said they were a turn-on.

The music industry in the mid-nineties was a fairly testosterone-heavy place. The United States was experiencing the fallout of the grunge era and in Britain, Brit Pop, which was colorful and optimistic, though a bit sexist (the Gallagher brothers of Oasis noted their opinion of women as "birds are rubbish"), ruled. Lad magazines—a cross between a porn magazine and a traditional men's magazine—like *Loaded*, *FHM*, and *Maxim* were also on the rise in the United Kingdom, and, eventually, in the United States. The Spice Girls were welcomed with typical hyperbole by the British music press: the industry paper *Music Week* wrote, "Just when boys with guitars threaten to rule pop life an all-girl, in-yer-face pop group has arrived with enough sass to burst that rockist bubble!!" Too bad they were preconceived and prepackaged.

For all their "ordinariness" in the natural talent department, each woman was attractive and sexy, which, combined with a boisterous but unthreatening message of female unity, proved to be incredibly successful. Their debut album, simply called *Spice*, sold 18 million copies around the world and hit number one in thirty countries. An eleven-week, forty-city North American tour averaged 99 percent capacity, with 720,000 Americans and Canadians making a pilgrimage to see the group in person. According to *Brandweek*, the average concertgoer spent an additional fifteen dollars on merchandise. One marketing executive estimated that "on this basis it's fair to predict a total income of $1 billion."

The Spice brand was further used to sell everything from Walkers potato chips to Chupa Chup lollipops to Cadbury candy to wallpaper to a video game, which sold 75,000 units in its first two months. There was even a limited-edition fragrance called Impulse Spice. ("Impulse Spice was deliberately created to reflect the new trend for 'girl power,'" Graziela Calfat, Elida Faberge's European innovations manager, told one reporter. "We saw the benefits of a fragrance that could be positioned as young, independent, modern and individual.") As part of the "Generation Next" campaign, a CD single was released exclusively through Pepsi. Customers could redeem twenty pull-tabs off their soft drinks for the single and a chance to see the group perform in Turkey. Six hundred thousand consumers redeemed the offer, equaling about 12 million cans sold. This kind of marketing was such a success at least in part because of how young the Spice Girls' fan base skewed. According to an American Psychological Association (APA) report from 2007 on the sexualization of girls, very young children are the most susceptible to marketing, and it's not until after eight years old that they can distinguish between regular TV programming and commercials designed to sell them something.

The group was so successful that Prince Charles suggested he might consider taking over as their manager. But they weren't untouchable. Ginger Spice was lambasted by the media when, on a tour of South Africa, she likened Nelson Mandela's struggle to girl power, saying that, while some might find her claim arrogant, "everyone has their fight for freedom, and this is our little quest. I've read his biography, and he admires anyone that's fighting for a cause. The only comparison between us is triumph over adversity." Halliwell, to her credit, has a point; though the five women were hardly poster girls for struggling and the quote is a bit blithe, the fight for global women's rights is certainly a valid one. But while Ginger was the political Spice, she was hardly Gloria Steinem. Nelson Mandela, for his part, was quoted as saying that meeting them was "one of the greatest moments of my life," though it's hard to say if he respected their politics or their pop songs.

Their version of girl power was even described by the BBC as a "social phenomenon" because of the young girls who embraced the Spice Girl paradigm of getting what you want, placing an importance on female friendship, and being positive. In *The Observer*, the comedian David Walliams said, "Not everyone has read *The Female Eunuch*, but everyone's heard of Geri Halliwell saying 'Girl Power.'" The author Ryan Dawson wrote, "The Spice Girls changed British culture enough for Girl Power to now seem completely unremarkable."

The group's philosophy also had its supporters in the United States. The *Bust* editor Debbie Stoller told *The Seattle Times* in 1998,

> One of the worst messages that we give to teen girls all the time is, now that you're a teenage girl you're going to have to say no to everything . . . It's all about controlling your desires, your urges. Silly nail polishes and glittery things are a little crack in the culture that's saying to girls, it's OK to say yes to something. Girls should have a chance to be girls. I asked a lot of little girls,

what do the Spice Girls mean to you? What does girl power mean to you? And the answers that they gave me were straight out of *Our Bodies, Ourselves* . . . That we're as good as boys, and sometimes better. It means that your friends will always be there for you, no matter what happens. That made me think, well, [the Spice Girls are] a silly brand of feminism for older teens. But if this is feminism-lite, kind of a junior edition, that's just the right size for little girls.

The Spice Girls had plenty of fans beyond the training-bra years too. Marcelle Karp went to see their movie *Spice World* with a huge posse of thirtysomething friends when it opened in New York City. "The audience was thirteen-year-old girls. We were the oldest people in there, basically," she says with a laugh. She was drawn to the group because she thought that they achieved a lot with their girl-power message. "Feminism at the end of the day is to believe that girls and boys are of equal value and there's no easy way to explain that to a five-year-old. The Spices say that girls rule, your friends come first, and I thought that was a very important message to kids. Girl power, feminism, it's all under the same umbrella."

One scene in *Spice World* includes a military-style cheer: "We're the Spice Girls, yes indeed, just girl power is all we need. We know how we got this far, strength and courage and a Wonderbra . . . listen up, take my advice, we need five for the power of spice . . . give it up, give it out, take a stand, take a shout, one, two, three, four, five, Spice Girls!" Their take on feminism was heavy on the sisterhood and the inherent badass-ness of being a girl— and the Spices should be lauded for that message.

Whether or not the Spice Girls were good for feminism, or

were feminists themselves, is a debate that even feminists cannot agree on. Karp wrote in *Bust*, "Let [the Spice Girls] get up on MTV or in the movies and remarket feminism and call it girl power. Put that out there, let the girls soak it up and think about what girl power really means." And reenvisioning feminism was certainly a proposed goal of the Spices, who saw the social movement as lacking in currency by the time they got on the scene. In their book, they took on the F-word head-on: "Feminism has become a dirty word. Girl Power is just a nineties way of saying it. We can give feminism a kick up the arse. Women can be so powerful when they show solidarity." Geri Halliwell appeared not to have warmed up to feminism any further or understood it more deeply in a 2007 interview where she dismissed the movement with a few shopworn clichés: "[Feminism is] about labeling. For me feminism is bra-burning lesbianism. It's very unglamorous. I'd like to see it rebranded. We need to see a celebration of our femininity and softness."

Although the Spice Girls claimed to know what girls really, really wanted, they created no Spice scholarships, no high-profile foundations to actualize girl power beyond just a catchphrase. At the same time, those are lofty expectations for a band—no one would expect such activism from the Rolling Stones. But bands like U2 have successfully combined political activism with international fame. The Spice Girls could have taken a cue from Coldplay or Lilith Fair the decade before and at least invited nonprofit organizations along on tour with them. The Spices were outspoken, but their messages were shallow at best, celebrating getting it on ("2 Become 1"), the fraught relationship between mothers and daughters ("Mama"), and having a good time ("Spice Up

Your Life"). Confessional songwriting this was not, let alone a call to action.

But wouldn't they have shown a little bit more solidarity if they had at least called themselves feminists? The feminist activist Jennifer Pozner was more dismissive, writing that it was "probably a fair assumption to say that a 'zigazig-ha' is not Spice shorthand for 'subvert the dominant paradigm.'" Girl power is a safe barometer of one's comfort level with the word "girl" itself. The preference for "woman" (or, for the more dedicated gender essentialists, "womyn") over "girl" was often a generational divider. For third wave feminists, "girl" was a reclamation of your outspoken and unself-conscious youth instead of all that was diminutive and infantilizing. The problem with girl power Spice-style was not the "girl" but the "power"; the addition of "power" implies that "girl" isn't powerful enough on its own.

The simplification of punk rock, third wave feminist values to girl power was a shocking concept to the riot grrrl veteran Tobi Vail. "When I hear a Spice Girls song on the radio, it is profoundly alienating," she says. "I might be like, 'Wow, this is cool,' but then I go, 'Isn't it a little fucked up?' And am I crazy, or did I make this happen?" She asks an important question: Would the Spice Girls have existed without riot grrrl? On the surface, yes—a manufactured girl group singing about love and friendship was certainly nothing groundbreaking. But I don't believe their message of girl power would have existed without riot grrrl predating them by a few years. Whoever masterminded the Spices' girl-power message in the mid-nineties conceivably heard or read about riot grrrl. Even in the United Kingdom, the movement was on magazine covers. Shampoo and Helen Love, a Welsh group whose song "Formula

One Racing Girls" included a chant of "girl power," were both fairly well-known indie groups who took the riot grrrl message and borrowed it for their own poppier songs. But neither of those bands became more than historical footnotes and the media hadn't covered riot grrrl much since the 1992 blackout. Those four years created the cultural space for the riot grrrl ideals to resurface beyond the white, middle-class, university-educated set.

Previous fusions of music and feminism in the nineties like riot grrrl or foxcore were much more unfiltered than anything the Spice Girls ever did or said, so it's worth asking if the Spice Girls' message of smiley-faced feminism for the masses did more for girl liberation than Bikini Kill's rage. For Jennifer Baumgardner, the Spice Girls' accessibility gave them more reach and thus the ability to get their feminist message (however watered down) to a broader and younger audience who would have been alienated by the form riot grrrl's message took. "I saw little girls dancing to the Spice Girls who really did imagine themselves as the stars of this show as opposed to the bit players. Bikini Kill didn't sound enough like the Disney Channel," says Baumgardner.

In *Manifesta*, Amy Richards and Jennifer Baumgardner's defining book on third wave feminism, they write about "the danger that Spice Girls Pencil Set Syndrome will settle in: girls buying products created by male-owned companies that capture the slogan of feminism, without the power." Perhaps the greatest contradiction in the Spicified worldview was the ease of its messageless message; simply wearing a pink baby tee emblazoned with the words GIRL POWER became an effortless way to declare your allegiance, and the meaning behind the words became depoliticized and diluted to the point that they became just another faddish catchphrase.

The Spice Girls enabled girls not to use their collective power to realize actual change in the world, but to accumulate Spice merchandise; this wasn't feminism as much as it was girl-targeted consumerism. Vail's former bandmate Hanna described her own fears about girl power as such in *Manifesta*:

> The thing that disturbs me now, with commercialization, is I fear that young girls will be encouraged to stop there, that young girls will go buy their Spice Girls notebook and not go to the library or the gay or feminist bookstores. But, deep down, I think people are smarter than that and when they experience girl power in the real form, they'll get excited and seek out more information.

What the Spice Girls lacked, like Alanis Morissette, was a way for their adherents to practice the feminism the musicians preached. Without zine- or songwriting workshops or grassroots networks of any kind, a girl who felt radicalized by girl power could theoretically enact feminist principles by running for school office, speaking up in class, creating artwork, writing a novel, or just living with confidence. But the easiest and most obvious way was to acquire Spice-branded merchandise. In the Spice world, all it took to be one of them was to dance and sing along, but that was also its flaw—you had to buy into the world.

The Spice Girls did exert independence where they seemed to think it mattered the most: their own careers. In 1997, they fired their manager, Simon Fuller (his was their second firing, after they dumped their initial managers, the Herberts; Fuller has gone on to create the *Idol* series, including *American Idol*), winning a certain kind of independence that Halliwell called "actual girl power in action. We've shown we do take our business seriously and we take our destinies into our own hands. We've always taken responsibility for everything we've done. It's obviously very unsettling for male-dominated newspapers to realize that five women in short skirts have got a brain."

The Spice Girls' encouragement of sassy, unladylike behavior—like growling at the camera and kung fu kicking—was just as alluring to marketers as it was to young girls. "Marketers see that they now have the ability to reach four-, five- and six-year-old girls in a way that they never have been before," Paul Kurnit, president of the marketing and advertising agency Griffin Bacal, told *KidScreen*, a trade publication. "The whole girl power thing lends itself well to marketing even if, and when, the Spice Girls themselves no longer exist," said Steve Grubbs, an ad executive, in the same article, where he also cites ads using female athletes instead of the male athletes who would have once dominated. By embracing the grrrl side of girl power, tomboys like Sporty Spice were proving they were just as sexually desirable as more feminine girls, creating a new archetype—woman as warrior—to market to girls.

Lady Footlocker ran an ad in the late nineties featuring an alterna-cover of Helen Reddy's "I Am Woman," and around the same time, Mountain Dew ran a similar ad with a punk rendition of Maurice Chevalier's patronizing "Thank Heaven for Little Girls." (It was sung by Lesley Rankine, formerly of the foxcore band Silverfish, who had a memorable band T-shirt emblazoned with the slogan HIPS, TITS, LIPS, POWER.) A writer in *The Village Voice* describes the commercial, which cuts between Rankine's shaved head spitting out the lyrics and footage of extreme sports enthusiasts like Picabo Street: "As they take the plunge, they each let loose a savage girl-holler—the kind of roar you might hear in a Hole or Bikini Kill song, but stripped of anger and transformed into purely joyous exuberance." The commercial ends with blissed-out boys cooing, "I think I'm in love." That detail, like the girl power of the Spice Girls, is a crucial point, because it asserts that a woman can be as kick-ass as she wants, but she must still be conventionally attractive, marketable, and—most paramount of all—a suitable object of affection. Once muscular female athletes, like the Williams sisters in tennis, became famous on a national level, and began appearing on the cover of *Vogue*, being an attractive woman became a little bit harder—one now had to be toned, as well as slim and pretty.

Girl power was such an easily communicable message that Posh, Baby, Ginger, Scary, and Sporty became unnecessary vessels for it. In 2001, the group split up, ostensibly to focus on their individual careers. Posh famously married the soccer star David Beckham, got breast implants, and moved to Los Angeles. Fashion has become her true calling (for which she removed her breast implants), and she's admitted in interviews that she was never the best singer or dancer. It's ironic that Posh, who was voted least identifiable by elementary-school-age fans (Sporty and Baby were the most), became the most famous. While Ginger did supposedly find enough fault with the group's lack of politics to quit in 1998—the Spices went on as a foursome—and became a United Nations Goodwill Ambassador, she later admitted an eating disorder and made a failed attempt at acting in America. Scary showed up in the tabloids after she became pregnant with Eddie Murphy's child and then appeared on the reality program *Dancing with the Stars*. Sporty had a minor hit in gay clubs with "I Turn to You," and Baby had similarly tepid success in Britain with her solo albums. Each of them became mothers.

All the hand-wringing over the Spice Girls may have been un-
founded. In 1998, at the height of the Spice social phenomenon,
the first academic study of the group was performed by the University of York. The researchers, who did the fieldwork at local
schools with girls ages six to eight, found that the sexual over-
tones went over the heads of children (something that is hard to
believe would be true for young fans of Britney Spears or the
Pussycat Dolls), and, according to a story on the study in the *Chicago Sun-Times*, this suggested that "the group triggers only a
'feel-good' belief in sticking up for themselves." Ann Kaloski, one
of the researchers, found that "what young girls seem to want
from the Spice Girls isn't an excuse to spend money or try to be
like them. They see them as an affirmation of what they already
have in themselves—they are fun, feisty and within reach." When
asked what they would want if a magic wand sprinkled them with
"Girl Power," the girls' ambitions strayed far from the superfici-
alities of wanting to be attractive to boys, but instead included
winning swimming races and being able to do backflips. The
Spices were credited with raising the expectations and aspirations
of girls; the BBC called this demographic the "can-do girls," who
were, for the first time in England, getting better A-level results
than their male counterparts. A 2006 article in *The Guardian*
contends that as the generation of eight-year-olds who listened to
"Wannabe" was turning eighteen, the Spice Girls' brand of brash
and unapologetic independence and promotion of sisterhood
succeeded in giving girls an early taste of feminism. In her 2000
work *The Whole Woman*, Germaine Greer cites a 1998 study of
children's oral culture that found that "whereas half the space in
school playgrounds used to be taken up by a self-selecting group
of boys playing [soccer], girls' clapping and dancing games were

taking over"—and the researchers attribute that shift at least partly to the Spice Girls' influence.

But empowerment doesn't equal feminism. *Venus* magazine's founder, Amy Schroeder, interacts with the college-age girls who are her readers or the interns at the magazine. "It's interesting because I ask them if they consider if they're feminist and they're not necessarily calling themselves feminists—some of them are even women's studies majors!—but so much of what they do is feminist," says Schroeder. "I think they are products of the Spice Girls generation; they're strong women, really creative and confident, they know that they can do what they can to make it and succeed in the workplace." Alison Piepmeier thinks her students have a subconscious feminism. "They have an expectation that they're going to be able to do what they want to do with their lives. That level of expectation of the world—I have things to say, I have things to accomplish, the world needs to listen to me— makes me think that having been raised in a culture with rhetoric about girl power did have an impact on them."

But she is hesitant to wholeheartedly embrace an idea that existed mostly as a slogan emblazoned across body-hugging baby tees, printed on pots of glitter lip gloss, or found in the sexy-but-sassy megasuccessful line of Bratz dolls. "The marketing machine was so quick to jump on the third wave [of feminism]," Piepmeier points out. "It's one of the things that differentiates it from earlier versions of feminism, when we didn't have the kind of tech culture that allowed ideas to be communicated so quickly."

Others who supported certain aspects of girl power had their doubts about it as well. The same 2006 article in *The Guardian* that praises the five women for introducing feminism to the playground also connects the Spice Girls to the eroticization of girlhood: "Here, it was alleged, was post-feminism revealed as a busted flush: five supposedly empowered starlets whose diminutive nicknames and push-up bras suggested patriarchal business as usual. Extending the logic of that argument, you might even charge them with responsibility for the wave of raunch culture."

As defined by Ariel Levy in her book *Female Chauvinist Pigs*, raunch culture is women making sex objects of other women and of themselves. It's "empowering" (a word increasingly becoming devoid of all meaning) women to wear a shirt with the *Hustler* logo, call all her friends "bitch," or get an eighty-dollar Brazilian wax. "Sex appeal," Levy writes, "has become a synecdoche of all appeal." Raunch culture took the third wave ideas of using your sexuality to be powerful and sexual ownership and replaced them with consumerism. It fed into tired virgin/whore stereotypes and didn't do a thing for sisterhood.

Raunch culture falls into a recent larger trend that encouraged adult women to act more childlike and children to act more like grown women. Young girls are being marketed to more than ever before, with annual sales of personal care products for teens and tweens estimated at $8 billion in 2009. In 2007, Nair released its Pretty line, which is targeted at ten-to-fifteen-year-old "first time hair removers" with green-apple-scented waxes and the tagline "Pretty isn't a look, it's a feeling." In Australia, the website girl.com.au, which is read mostly by girls nine to fourteen, ran a feature about Brazilian waxes that included the sentence "Nobody really likes hair in their private regions and it has a childlike appeal." In 2004, Victoria's Secret launched its hypersuccessful Pink line of dog-printed panties and logo bras, banking on the notion that tween girls would want to mimic their older sisters— and making $500 million in sales during its first year alone. Bratz attempted to put out a line of branded padded bras sized for six-year-olds at Target Australia until parents protested. The British department store BHS sold a Little Miss Naughty range of bras and underwear starting in sizes for seven-year-olds. Tesco, another British chain, offered a Peekaboo Pole Dancing Kit in their toys and games aisle (their claim: "Now every girl can be a pole dancer!"). It came complete with a tiny garter and toy money to stuff in it. Girl-power T-shirts devolved into over-the-top tees for girls with slogans such as I'M TOO PRETTY TO DO MATH; WHO NEEDS A BRAIN WHEN YOU HAVE THESE? or NO MEANS NO accompanied, at the bottom, by, WELL, MAYBE IF I'M DRUNK. (David & Goliath, the company that manufactured the NO MEANS NO tee, pulled it after readers of a feminist blog complained. As a totally insulting apology, it offered a 10 percent discount on its MISS BITCH T-shirt. The password for the deal? "GIRL POWER!") Raunch wasn't just for sorority sister types. SuicideGirls has created an empire (including a radio show, burlesque tour, DVD, and book) by combining softcore porn with indie aesthetics. With their pigtails and tattoos, the models look like riot grrrls, but they derive their supposed power from posing nude for nominal fees.

The Spices can't be blamed entirely—their girl power had a sheen of innocence and optimism entirely absent from the *Girls Gone Wild* videos and pole dancing workshops that have become raunch hallmarks. But they proved that a young, female demographic was ready and willing to become consumers, and that a feminist-lite message like girl power was an effective method of marketing to them.

4.

POP TARTS

By the late nineties, a decade that had begun with a battle cry—a Democrat in office! a return to activism! girls in combat boots singing about sexual violence!—was ending with a sigh of resignation. For Sub Pop's Megan Jasper, the turn of the millennium was an odd time for music. "Our economy was really strong, the biggest problem was that our president got a blow job, the world seemed like it was in a decent place," she says. The problem was that prosperity doesn't create the most fertile ground for rebellion. "It was a good space, but there isn't that struggle or that thing that makes us hungry for something else. People felt like they needed some stability and to slow down for a change. During those times you see things soften."

Nineteen ninety-eight was the year *Titanic* swept the Oscars, Viagra went on sale, and Britney Spears was introduced to the world. In October of that year, Spears, a sixteen-year-old former Mouseketeer, released her debut single, ". . . Baby One More Time." The song, about the wish to reconcile a relationship—the chorus begged her lover to "hit me baby one more time"—became an instant classic. It was a perfect pop confection: catchy, hummable, and impossible to forget. In the video, Spears cast herself as the world's sexiest schoolgirl, wearing pigtails, a teeny kilt, and a blouse that barely buttoned over her chest—a stylistic choice she was said to have made herself. The song was a number one hit in America and equally big internationally, where it topped the charts in more than a dozen countries. Upon hearing it for the first time, Tori Amos declared the end of the female singer-songwriter era.

At least, that's the rumor. But it's not hard to believe; it did feel like a cohort of pop princesses—Britney, Christina, Jessica, Mandy, all seemingly interchangeable—had taken over the world. Collectively, they were blond, bland, sexy-but-virginal (or so they said), sang bubblegum pop songs, and were often backed by corporate America. They were more brands than artists.

Within just a few years of her debut, Britney Spears was ranked by *Forbes* as the world's most powerful celebrity, with ad campaigns and endorsements for Pepsi and McDonald's and a signature perfume. She also had a starring role in the movie *Crossroads*, in which she goes searching for her long-absent mother and makes a ton of money doing a poor karaoke rendition of Joan Jett's "I Love Rock-n-Roll." Her domination was unavoidable.

Spears's closest competition was the platinum blond, red-lipped Christina Aguilera, another alumna of the Mickey Mouse Club, who sang "What a Girl Wants" (the answer: boys). Even as teenagers, their roles in American culture were set: Britney was the sweet, dim, slightly naughty girl next door whose albums every parent would let their ten-year-old have, while Christina was molded in the Madonna school of pop stardom, all sexual agency and dance beats.

Besides the ubiquitous Spears and Aguilera, there was Mandy Moore, who was the least plastic of the pop princesses and, perhaps because of that fact, was arguably the least successful of them all. Moore started to get halfway decent reviews only when she switched to acting, starring in *A Walk to Remember* as a high school student who wants to get married before she dies of cancer. Rounding out the pop tart invasion was Jessica Simpson, a Baptist who bears a striking resemblance to Barbie. As a kind of fourth-place winner in the teen pop pantheon, her defining factor was her purity. Her father was a Baptist minister turned manager who gave her a creepy silver chastity ring when she was twelve. It was a virginity pledge that she apparently maintained until her (now defunct) marriage to the former boy-band member Nick Lachey.

If the pop tart invasion was typified by empty blond shells of marketable womanhood, the late nineties boy band trend, which included 98 Degrees (Lachey's group), 'N Sync, and the Backstreet Boys, was the male version, reducing men to buff but coiffed sensitive jocks in wind-flapping unbuttoned silk shirts. It was truly an era that favored style over substance.

Simpson, who had languished at the bottom rung of the pop crop, brilliantly leveraged her marriage to Lachey into superstardom. In 2003, *Newlyweds: Nick and Jessica*, a reality show about the Lachey-Simpson marriage, began its first season on MTV. On its pilot episode, Simpson asks, of the Chicken of the Sea brand tuna she's consuming, "Is this chicken, what I have, or is this fish?" cementing her place as the nation's most treasured dimwit. How much of the ditzy blond role was an act is up for debate, but

Simpson milked her newfound fame for all it was worth, posing on the cover of *Rolling Stone* in November 2003 wearing an undershirt, floral panties, heels, and a lot of fake tan under the headline "Housewife of the Year." She wasn't the only star who was in a hurry to settle down. Britney Spears and Christina Aguilera also married young.

With their small-town upbringings, discoveries on TV competitions or childrens' shows, enviable wardrobes, and perfect romances, pop stars were becoming the late-nineties embodiment of fairy-tale princesses, rich girls who don't work beyond showing up to balls in sparkly gowns and managing a cadre of handsome suitors. I can't help but imagine the boy bands of the era in those roles—queuing up for a spot on their dance cards. It doesn't sound like such a bad life. In a *New York Times Magazine* story on princess culture, Peggy Orenstein writes, "If nothing else, Princess [has] resuscitated the fantasy of romance that that era of feminism threatened, the privileges that traditional femininity conferred on women despite its costs—doors magically opened, dinner checks picked up, Manolo Blahniks. Frippery. Fun." Bolstered by the popularity of its own branded princesses— that's Cinderella, Snow White, Sleeping Beauty, Ariel, Belle, Jasmine, Pocahontas, and Mulan—Disney, a company known for heightening the passivity of the princesses from their original fairy tales, began producing a line of more than 25,000 Disney Princess items, which has become a $4 billion industry. Everyone else marketing to young girls jumped on the princess bandwagon: princess Barbies, princess makeovers at the tween chain Club Libby Lu. According to Orenstein, Club Libby Lu's malls are chosen based on their sales potential by a company formula called the Girl Power Index.

Professor Lyn Mikel Brown has done research on the princess phenomenon as well. "It's easy to start with the feminist role model because girl power is so marketable, but expand that to include everything pink and princesses." She uses the example of the *Shrek* movies, which have the ostensible message of beauty being found on the inside. But of the franchise's more than eighty licensing agreements, none of them features the princess Fiona in her "ugly" ogre form. The feisty young adventuress Dora the Explorer is the star of an animated series on cable television that has been a hit with children since it first aired in 1999. Even precocious, bilingual Dora turned into a princess in a two-part story arc that led to a Magic Hair Fairytale Dora tie-in doll (a touch of the wand makes her hair grow). In 2009, the character was given a controversial makeover that replaced her backpack and shorts with platform sandals and a miniskirt.

Like so many shiny red apples proffered by witches in fairy tales, there is a little bit of poison hidden inside the princess paradigm. If there was real empowerment behind princesses, they'd be a powerful tool for girls' self-actualization. A princess is special, but her uniqueness is always discovered by another character; she never finds it within herself. Princess narratives say that women can't be princesses without society-approved standards of beauty and a prince to save them. As pop stars morph into real-life versions of royalty, with fantastic, untenable standards of fancy clothes and cars and perfect bodies and relationships, we get further from any hint of real-life vulnerability, no matter how many times *US Weekly* tries to prove that stars are "just like us" because they pump their own gas. (Previous generations of pop stars might have been household names, but the minutiae of their daily lives were never so dissected as with the pop tarts.) As any tabloid reader knows, celebrities are rewarded with coverage for playing to their brand's stereotype, providing us an easily identifiable story arc to follow: who we're to pity, who we're to root for, who's on the road to redemption. It's no wonder that so many child stars end up in rehab or obscurity—they're pushed into tightly defined roles before they even know who they are.

One of the fights of third wave feminism has been to let rebel girls embrace their inner princesses—after all, Courtney Love did show up to the Oscars in a tiara paired with a vintage slip dress in 1995. But it's worth noting that some of the most truly powerful music of the nineties was not about princesses, but queens. Evelyn McDonnell decries "princess tyranny," as she calls it in her book *Mamarama*. "Our leaders didn't sing of princesses," she writes, mentioning that the Runaways, the teen rock band that launched Joan Jett's career, billed themselves as the Queens of Noise. Jett produced Bikini Kill's anthemic "Rebel Girl," which included a nod to "the queen of my world." Bratmobile had a song called "Queenie," and so did PJ Harvey, with "50 Foot Queenie." And there's the rapper Queen Latifah, who sang "I bring wrath to those who disrespect me like a dame" in her 1994 crossover hit "U.N.I.T.Y."

The late-nineties twist on princesses was to add a sexual gloss to the phenomenon. In the APA's report on the sexualization of girls, the Disney Corporation was singled out for remaking characters like Ariel and Pocahontas with a new, sexy identity: more cleavage, less clothing. Music was no different. As someone who was in elementary school during the last female teen idol boom in the mid-eighties, I find the pop stars in retrospect laughably modest. "You go back and you look at those videos and you see Debbie Gibson and Tiffany and there's two inches of their midriff and turtlenecks," says the writer Wendy McClure. "They looked Mormon." Even Madonna's now infamous performance of "Like a Virgin" at the inaugural 1984 MTV Video Music Awards with her writhing onstage, dressed in a belt buckle that spelled out BOY TOY, garters, and a wedding dress seems, in retrospect, fairly chaste. Though the nineties crop of pop starlets had devout Christians in the bunch—beliefs oft cited, particularly in the early careers of Simpson and Spears—their taste in apparel didn't tend toward the unrevealing.

Spears's fans, like Ariel Feldman, a writer and student who was in grade school in the late nineties, loved her look. "Britney came out and I remember her vinyl jumpsuit and lots of makeup and thinking, 'Oh my God, this girl's so cool,'" Feldman says. "'She's like a sex maniac! She's so different from anything I've ever seen.'" She sees the attraction as a phase. "From ten or eleven, you want to look like that. In your head, you think you're sexy, but you have a prepubescent body. You're trying to look like you're twenty-five." Hilary Davis, who had been a Spice Girls fan early in her grammar school career, had to make a doll in her sixth-grade home economics class and made one of Spears—whom she recalls liking principally because her songs were upbeat and because, after listening to them a few times, she could sing along—in a half-shirt from Spears's "Sometimes" video. Racy styling had a role in the young pop stars' careers beyond provocation: it was a way to show their independence and maturation as artists.

The writer Lauren Waterman went to see Spears in Chicago in early 2002 with her boyfriend. "It was teenagers all dressed as Britney clones. I was looking at the mothers and thinking, 'I can't believe you let your daughter dress like that,'" she says. Fashion trends at the time included low-rise jeans and cropped shirts to show off the abdominal region, the body part that most defines the era. Our bellies, once bared as political canvases, became known as abs and they were supposed to be taut and covered in body glitter, not Sharpie. In 1999, a *Newsweek* cover story asked, "Tweens: Are They Growing Up Too Fast?" Girls who are "8 going on 25" were part of "a generation stuck in fast-forward, children in a fearsome hurry to grow up." Fashion, especially for pubescent girls, is girl power—it's one way of differentiating your taste from your parents' and taking control of your identity (and changing fashions inspire alarmist articles like *Newsweek*'s every few years). Parents could even potentially use risqué outfits and behavior from pop stars as a way to start a conversation about their daughters' sexual mores.

But in a society where being sexy is powerful, choosing to dress sexily becomes more compulsory and less of the authentic choice it was for Madonna, Courtney Love, or Kathleen Hanna. In the 1998 book *The Body Project: An Intimate History of American Girls*, Joan Jacobs Brumberg studied teen girls' diaries over a hundred years. In the last twenty years that she cataloged, from the late seventies to the late nineties, the focus of self-improvement was almost exclusively focused on changing their appearances, rather than their studies or likability. The APA report furthers this analysis, explaining that girls "internalize and reproduce within their own self-schemas this objectified perspective, an effect referred to as 'self-objectification,' which involves adopting a third person perspective on the physical self and constantly assessing one's own body in an effort to conform to the culture's standards."

But what if girls found an unlikely liberation in all that body exhibitionism? "A few years ago, I noticed that none of my students were coming to class wearing very much clothes," says the professor Gayle Wald. "They wore halter tops and flip-flops and seemed totally comfortable showing their stomachs. On the one hand, I thought, Wow, this is great: a body unself-consciousness that I'll never have. On the other hand, I thought it was another form of hyperexploitation, fashion's dictating that these girls wear no clothes. But the flip side is that these girls, despite the insistence in the media on perfection, feel a confidence to display their bodies frankly and without shame. There's something to that." Therein lies the upside to the kind of girl power that pop stars were perhaps unintentionally advocating. Showing off their stomachs was a kind of body confidence that could have been culled from riot grrrl zines, but found a much wider audience in Spears's or Aguilera's young fans.

The revealing clothing trend got carried even further as time progressed. The Pussycat Dolls, who were notable for wearing stockings, garters, and little else, in the name of "body confidence," were dubbed the new millennium's version of the Spice Girls. Except the group, which grew out of a Los Angeles burlesque troupe of the same name, made even the Spice Girls look like aging feminist revolutionaries. Robin Antin, the troupe's founder, named the group (if it could even be called that—I defy anyone to name all of them, or even to name any beyond the group leader, Nicole Scherzinger) thusly because she had a vision of, as she told *The New York Times* in 2006, "making everyone look like a real, living doll."

Ron Fair, the head of Interscope's A&M Records and one of the producers of the Pussycat Dolls' debut album, *PCD*, told *The New York Times* that the group's racy image read more mature to its younger fans. "Once it's branded as a tween thing, it's very hard to flip it up. But what the older sister and older brother like definitely trickles down to the kids. That's what's happening to the Pussycat Dolls." In early 2007, the reality TV show competition *The Search for the Next Pussycat Doll* ironically replaced the smarty-pants series *Veronica Mars* in the CW lineup. "It's about female empowerment, self-discovery and personal transformation," CW Entertainment's head Dawn Ostroff said of *The Search*. Girls besotted with the idea of becoming the group's seventh member gushed about how the Pussycat Dolls stand for female empowerment, but their hummable hit "Don't Cha" couldn't be further from feminism. The song's lyrics—"Don't cha wish your girlfriend was hot like me/Don't cha wish your girlfriend was a freak like me"—put forward the belief that a woman's worth lies solely in her appearance and sexual permissiveness and just furthers the notion that women are in competition with one another over men. But the Dolls weakly claim otherwise. "The song might say 'Don't cha wish your girlfriend was hot like me?' But the way we play on it is it's empowering for all women out there. We want them to feel like that," Scherzinger told MTV. "And when we perform it, all the girls in the audience are feeling it, and we always dedicate it to them." The idea that they represent power to some women is depressing and indicative that feminism still has a lot of ground to cover. But the responsibility to be, well, better is in the hands of the Dolls and their handlers. It seems unduly harsh to judge their fans.

Even pop stars who try to forge an identity outside the usual paradigm are often sucked into it. When Mikki Halpin, who was then working for *Seventeen* magazine, was dispatched to interview the rebellious pop-rocker Avril Lavigne, she doggedly tried to find out whether Lavigne was different from the pop star pack precisely because of the way she dressed. "She was saying, 'I'm so different from Britney. Britney's about sex appeal and exploiting her body and I don't,'" recalls Halpin, who pointed out that if the tiny Lavigne wore a size fourteen, she probably wouldn't have a record deal. Lavigne agreed but said, in her defense, that she was just trying to be herself. It's unclear how much of "herself" was really her personal style, but Lavigne was marketed as a kind of tomboy who stuck her tongue out at cameras and wore heavy black eyeliner. Her signature look revolved around pairing tank tops with neckties, and she sung songs about skater boys. She was ostensibly an outsider (though she was never really one; just read the lyrics to "Sk8tr Boi" to get a sense of her privilege: "I'm with the skater boy/I said see ya later boy/I'll be backstage after the show/I'll be at a studio/singing the song we wrote/About a girl you used to know"), but an outsider flavor of pop star, much in the way that Sporty Spice was the tomboy of the Spice Girls— just an easy way for girls to discern one pop star from another. In *Slate*, the music critic Jody Rosen called her "the female answer to all those mall-rat punk-pop bands—proof that a 17-year-old girl could whine and snarl just like the boys and look just as silly in a pair of pants five sizes too big."

But this break from tradition proved to be a mere Trojan horse. She was all pop star at heart with the hot body, catchy songs, and major label handlers to prove it. She wasn't exactly radicalized, either. When Halpin asked Lavigne if she was a feminist, the Canadian popster replied, "What's that?" Lavigne was young—not yet eighteen when her first album came out—but as the poster girl for that era's girl power (she was vaguely independent and sassy and had a certain ferocity) it was surprising that she had never even heard of the concept.

So Halpin explained that, to her, a feminist is someone who thinks women are equal to men. Lavigne's reaction was no doubt the result of encountering a subject her media coaches hadn't briefed her on: she told Halpin, "I don't know a lot about it so I don't really think that what you're saying sounds good." Halpin, who is genuinely interested in raising the political consciousness of teen girls (she later authored a book on teens and activism), took it upon herself to send Lavigne a copy of Jennifer Baumgardner and Amy Richards's *Manifesta*, hoping that a little history would make feminism sound better. Often while working at magazines, journalists end up interviewing celebrities again and again as they churn out new projects to promote. So Halpin got a chance a year later to see if Lavigne was ever able to fully apprise herself on the subject of feminism. She told Halpin she had read "some of it."

A teen pop star being ignorant of political movements is not terribly surprising. The far more disappointing role reversal came a few years later when Lavigne, after years of marketing herself as a rebel and an outsider (albeit on hollow terms), bleached her hair, spoke of her desire to marry, started wearing Chanel, was rumored to have had plastic surgery, and launched her own perfume.

The real bait and switch, though, isn't that Lavigne was really a girly girl underneath the heavy eyeliner and defiant posturing; it's that she advocates jealousy over sisterhood. Take the chorus to the hit song "Girlfriend," from her third album, *The Best Damn Thing*: "Hey! Hey! You! You!/I don't like your girlfriend!/No way! No way!/I think you need a new one." In the accompanying video, a rule-breaking rock 'n' roll girl and a prissy redhead, both played by Lavigne, compete for the love of the same guy—not a lot of girl unity to be found. This being Avril's universe, the viewer is supposed to root for the rebel and we're supposed to despise the preppy girl on the basis of her normalcy. The video ends on a perverse note, with the rebel Lavigne hitting a golf ball into the head of the square girl and stealing off with the guy. As Jody Rosen wrote in a *Slate* article called "Mean Grrrl"—the title an ironic conflation of two popular perceptions of angry young women, the mean girl and the riot grrrl—"Avril's rock 'n' roll high school seems a lot like every other godawful high school, only its evil alpha girls have jet-black hair and wear Ramones T-shirts."

Her "Girlfriend" lyrics also betray a different Lavigne than the rule-breaking punk of her video: "I think you know I'm damn precious/And hell yeah, I'm the motherfuckin' princess." *The Best Damn Thing* includes "One of Those Girls," wherein she derides predatory, money-hungry girls who will "take you for a ride and you'll be left with nothing/You'll be broken and she'll be gone/Off to the next one." She's still a rebel, but her rebellion is against other girls. Once the outsider, Lavigne proved herself to be the meanest girl of them all.

The shtick of the rebel who doesn't act like your garden-variety star had been explored before Lavigne's appearance by Pink, aka Alecia Beth Moore, who rose to fame when her debut album, *Can't Take Me Home*, went double platinum in 2000. She had trademark pink hair and a punky attitude while opening for 'N Sync. Pink has always maintained that she's different from the other crop of pop stars by virtue of her outspokenness. In concert in 2007 at Madison Square Garden she declared, "I have a lot of political opinions" as an intro to her song "Dear Mr. President." Her song "Stupid Girls" vilified the scourge of tabloid stars superseding smart, precocious young women. "What happened to the dreams of a girl president/She's dancing in the video next to 50 Cent," she sings, later praising "outcasts and girls with ambition," two things rarely lauded in pop music or pop culture.

But instead of providing a cultural critique of why girls would think that playing the *Girls Gone Wild* or ditzy blond card is the best way to get ahead, Pink's judgment falls harder on individual girls than on society. It's most evident in the "Stupid Girls" video, where tanning, owning small dogs, having large breasts, and shopping at expensive boutiques are all deemed to be systemic of the dumbing down of girl culture.

And in the end, the video is hypocritical: Pink gets almost as naked as Paris Hilton got in that grainy video of hers. Faux sisterhood is nothing to be proud of, but neither is playing the mean girl, which only reinscribes tiresome notions of girls as catty, competitive, and jealous of one another. So, even though Pink's song is a much needed corrective—and in user reviews in places like iTunes and Amazon, hundreds of girls effuse over it—it's hardly subversive.

It's interesting to compare the dogmatic messages of Pink and Lavigne with that of Gwen Stefani, of the nouveau-ska band No Doubt, who successfully leveraged pop stardom by appealing to (and not alienating) her female fans. This was a woman who played fast and free with her girlhood, who mocked anyone who would belittle her in No Doubt's 1995 hit "Just a Girl." Though Gwen Stefani may have been the only female in a band of boys, and though she may have worn red lipstick and lacquered nails, her rendition of "Just a Girl" still raged against the patriarchy, "Oh . . . I've had it up to here!/Oh . . . am I making myself clear?/I'm just a girl/I'm just a girl in the world . . ./That's all that you'll let me be!" There was a sense that she was performing for her teen girl fans alone.

The girl fighting that Lavigne and Pink encourage is an outgrowth of a phenomenon that the Colby College professor Lyn Mikel Brown calls "girl typing." There are two types of girls: those who are for the boys and those who are one of the guys. In other words, they could be pretty and playful (but vapid and trivial) and an object of affection for the boys, or they could be sensible and interesting (but asexual and responsible) and friends with the boys. Both types put boys at the center and don't encourage sisterhood. She cites "Girlfriend" and "Stupid Girls" as examples of the construction of girls putting down other girls. "It's boring but it sells like crazy because girls have incredible anxiety about these topics: being liked by boys and being left out by other girls," says Mikel Brown. "This kind of stuff sells because it's what girls are most anxious about." Girls are forced into choosing sides and, as a result, there's an implied message to these songs of tension and aggression.

But then something happened: the pop tarts began to grow up. We had watched the fairy-tale narrative of these girls' lives unfold, and with the constant monitoring of celebrity culture, we've also been able to see just how hard it is to maintain the happy ending. They got older; life got complicated, and each girl reacted in a wholly different way. Christina Aguilera released the body-positive single "Beautiful" (its chorus: "You are beautiful no matter what they say") and another, "Can't Hold Us Down," that encouraged the "girls around the world who've come across a man who don't respect your worth" to "shout louder." This was the dawn of a new Aguilera: one who began to wear THIS IS WHAT

A FEMINIST LOOKS LIKE T-shirts in mainstream magazine photo shoots, talked openly about her history of bisexuality and domestic abuse, contributed money to women's shelters, and analyzed her own role as a pawn of men in both her career and her personal life. In 2009, she even enlisted Kathleen Hanna's band, Le Tigre, to work on her next album. She was still playing to the male gaze, as the video for "Can't Hold Us Down" will attest to, but she nonetheless deserves kudos for coming out as a sincere feminist who differed from Spears in her personal politics, musicianship, and involvement in her own career. Of course, neither Spears nor Aguilera ever said they were similar—it's the press that likes to pit female artists against one another. The others, in smaller ways, followed suit: Jessica Simpson, annoying as ever, got divorced and at least dropped her sanctimonious virgin affect. Mandy Moore, in an effort to discard her bubblegum past, released an album covering songs by the likes of Blondie, Joni Mitchell, and Carly Simon. On the cover she's sitting in a meadow, accessorized with long bangs and a flower.

When it comes to Britney Spears, her rebellion has become something of a media obsession. Her many transgressions against pop singer business as usual include a wedding in Las Vegas to a childhood friend that lasted all of fifty-five hours before an annulment; a marriage to the rapper/model/backup-dancer/father-of-two-Kevin Federline; a reality series, *Britney and Kevin: Chaotic*, documenting the early days of their love affair; a wedding most notable for the matching warmup suits the wedding party wore, emblazoned with PIMPS for the groom's side and MAIDS for the bride's; a son, followed quickly by an appearance on the cover of *Harper's Bazaar* nude and pregnant with a second son, who was born in September 2006, just two days before her elder child's first birthday. By November 2006, Spears announced that she was divorcing Federline (who supposedly got the news via text message). The breakup of her marriage was greeted by her fans like a return to the Britney of yore: she would once again eschew Cheetos, Marlboros, and bad boys and reembrace God and the gym and a flat stomach.

Instead, she went full-tilt bad girl. She became a fixture on the LA club scene and was suddenly best friends with Paris Hilton, breaking pretty much every societal standard for appropriate behavior for new moms. She checked into rehab in Antigua, but checked out a day later, flew back to California, and shaved off all her hair. The head shaving was the nexus of much concern. For a woman to shave off the hair on her head is a radical move—it rejects traditional ideals of feminine beauty and leaves the shavee literally more vulnerable. Spears would only comment, "People shave their heads all the time." Soon she was wearing wigs to cover up her newly bald head and was back in rehab. Post-rehab, her behavior was just as erratic: photographed exiting a car wearing no underwear; attacking a paparazzo's car with an umbrella, and dating and possibly marrying another; and finally losing custody of her two children.

She appeared at the 2007 MTV Video Music Awards primed to make a comeback performance but instead stumbled through her dance moves as if in an Ambien (or worse) haze, looking uncomfortable and out of shape in a glittery bikini. Her next album, *Blackout*, had lyrics that reeked of self-awareness—"I'm Mrs. Lifestyles of the Rich and Famous/I'm Mrs. 'Oh my God, that Britney's shameless'"—but was received to mixed reviews.

In a 1987 *Rolling Stone* interview, Madonna had said: "People have this idea that if you're sexual and beautiful and provocative, then there's nothing else you could possibly offer . . . And while it may have seemed like I was behaving in a stereotypical way, at the same time, I was also masterminding it . . . I think that when people realized that, it confused them." Our culture seems to have a particularly hard time with the suggestion that female pop stars have agency. I'm not trying to say that Spears masterminded her career at any point—she has always, tragically, seemed to have overbearing handlers—but, despite her very public transgressions, she does seem to be far more self-aware than most critics are willing to give her credit for.

By 2008, Spears had been diagnosed by countless tabloid articles with various mental illnesses: depression, bipolar disorder, mild schizophrenia. She was involuntarily hospitalized for psychiatric evaluation more than once, and her estranged father was put in charge of her professional and personal life. By then, Tori Amos had weighed in. At an Australian concert she sang, "Britney, they set you up/But you drank from their cup/Britney, they set you up/Oh, but this is what it looks like, love/This is what it looks like/When a star falls down." Amos came off as a bit sanctimonious, but she was at least showing more sympathy for the tarnished star than she had in the ". . . Baby One More Time" era.

Spears made her official comeback at 2008's MTV Video Music Awards, winning three moon man awards. In the concerts for her 2009 Circus tour, she chanted, "I don't know what you've been told/This mama is in control." Standing in the crowd, I believed in her redemption. But she will likely always be remembered for raising the bar on what constitutes shocking celebrity behavior. Fingers have been pointed in any number of directions—at the teams of paparazzi who follow her every move, the tabloid magazines that feign concern for her while delighting in her missteps, the parents who effectively let her trade in her childhood for a career—but Spears's case only underlines the need for feminism in these young pop stars' lives. I wonder if things would have turned out differently for her if, instead of being a vessel for the mainstream, she had learned how to rebel more constructively through music, like so many adolescents do. What would have happened if, rather than being the locus of a juggernaut dedicated to staying virginal and looking sexy and singing about boys, she had discovered the Slits or Hole or Ani DiFranco? Upon Spears's divorce, Tobi Vail inquired if there was any way to send her the Bikini Kill discography. With no apparent friends or confidantes, Spears, like so many alienated girls, could have at least found some comfort in music. Her acting out in her twenties most likely grew from the teen angst she had never been allowed to show, and this music could have served it.

While the late-nineties crop of pop stars was busy becoming adults, a new set emerged. The same demographic that, in previous generations, made a hit of Bratz dolls and Britney Spears has turned to Miley Cyrus, whose show, *Hannah Montana*, is a twist on the fantasy of becoming a star. In this case, Miley Stewart is by day an unpopular high school girl and by night superstar Hannah Montana (this being TV, all she has to do to mask her appearance is don a blond wig for her pop drag). As the show's theme song goes, she has "the best of both worlds." To listen to Miley Cyrus is, for the teen fan Ariel Feldman, to "have that feeling of I'm a girl, so what? I feel like I can do anything, like being a girl won't hinder anything." Marcelle Karp's daughter, Ruby, is "completely addicted" to the Disney oeuvre and even though Karp herself is the kind of cool mom who grew up attending punk shows, she doesn't judge her daughter's heroines. "I can't remember who was my Hannah Montana as a kid but I'm really glad that Ruby has one," she says. "Hannah Montana is flawed and she's wonderful and she's adorable and she's a good person—and that's a positive message to girls." Cyrus's blend of goofiness and self-confidence has a lot to like: she break-danced on the Teen Choice Awards, hangs out with the Obama girls, and has a song called "Nobody's Perfect." As Mary Elizabeth Williams wrote on *Salon*, "I like to think we aging riot grrrls see a little of ourselves in the spirited, boundaries- and decibels-shattering Hannah/Miley, and, we hope, in our daughters." (By 2006, teen girls were doing so well—catching up to boys on the SAT and often outscoring them, so that the girl crisis of the beginning of the decade that spurred *Reviving Ophelia* and Take Your Daughter to Work Day was looking conquered—that it created a kind of massive cultural anxiety, and an alleged "boy crisis" made headlines from *Newsweek* to *The Washington Post*. In 2008, a report called "Where the Girls Are: The Facts About Gender Equity in Education" by the American Association of University Women refuted the so-called crisis, finding that family income, not gender, is linked to academic success. The "boy crisis" was, once again, a backlash to all the gains that girls had made.)

Cyrus is the biggest, but not the only, emergent pop star. There's also Demi Lovato, Selena Gomez, Miranda Cosgrove, the various stars of the *High School Musical* franchise, and a seemingly infinite succession of others. I know that when I hear "White Horse," by Taylor Swift, a teen country sensation who crossed into the world of mainstream pop in 2007, I feel optimistic that she's already steering a generation of girls in the right direction. In it, Swift sings about a failed relationship, but instead of hoping for her Prince Charming to, yes, ride up on a white horse to rescue her, she subverts the fairy tale. "Cause I'm not your princess/ This ain't a fairy tale/I'm gonna find someone some day, who might actually treat me well," she sings. "This is a big world/That was a small town/there in my rearview mirror disappearing now/ And it's too late for you and your white horse to/catch me now."

In some ways, they're just business as usual. They have corporate ties—all of them are associated with corporations like Disney or Nickelodeon and have major endorsement deals—and they're traditionally beautiful and slender, but they're also a more racially and musically diverse group than Spears and company. What's most promising is a joyful, goofy approach to girlhood that feels more closely aligned to the Spice Girls' girl-power anthems than Jessica Simpson's balladeering.

It will be exciting to watch their careers to see if artistic maturation becomes shorthand for a sexier persona; this already seems to be the case for Cyrus. In spring 2008, snapshots of her flashing a neon green bra appeared online, followed shortly by an Annie Leibovitz photo shoot for *Vanity Fair* in which Cyrus posed in a bed sheet and little else. She posted mean-spirited parodies of rival Disney stars Demi Lovato and Selena Gomez on YouTube over that summer, and in early 2009, photos surfaced of the star making a slanty-eyed pose in a photograph with an Asian friend.

While these indiscretions betray some poor judgment and cultural insensitivity, Cyrus, like Spears before her, is ultimately guilty of weathering growing pains. The sixteen-year-old's rebellious streak is part of any standard-issue American adolescence; she's a teenager testing the boundaries of her smiley-faced Disney persona and trying on one a little more racy.

In one of two apologies on her website over the racist photo scandal, she wrote that "the press is trying to make me out as the new 'BAD GIRL!'" And she's right to feel vilified. Pop culture, especially when it comes to female stars, is stuck in a tired virgin-whore divide. Cyrus is offering up a more challenging version of female identity by taking a cue from her own show and leading a double life. She has placed herself firmly in a gray area between the "good" and "naughty" labels, refusing to settle in one camp. But she's not ducking labels as much as she is wearing as many of them as she desires, and all at the same time.

She has become a positive role model, following in the footsteps of musicians like Madonna and Cyndi Lauper who have successfully navigated a moral middle ground. Girls stand to learn more from flawed pop princesses than from wholly depraved or squeaky-clean ones. Cyrus and her cohort's fumbles not only make them more human, but also are universal to the teen experience. By being both good and bad—and wearing multiple labels—they are telling their young fans that they can't be limited to one stereotype. In the end, they get to be themselves.

5.

LADIES FIRST

By the new millennium, riot grrrl itself had became enough of a catchall phrase that, to this day, one can order a riot grrrl Halloween costume: a cheap red dress with vinyl spike details and a creepy vinyl studded belt with a skull buckle. The child models dressed in it are more often than not shown with chunky boots, pigtails, and angry-yet-come-hither expressions on their faces. The phrase had devolved into a synonym for angry young women, as in the chorus to "Riot Girl" by the mall punk band Good Charlotte: "My girl's a hot girl, a riot girl, and she's angry at the world."

The word "grrrl" was downgraded, as the nineties progressed, to a mere purr. In the cycle of language reappropriation, "grrrl" had given way to "grrl," which had, in turn, become a sassy synonym for "girl" even on websites like rightgrrl.com, whose target audience is women with an unabashed love not for bell hooks and the ERA, but for Margaret Thatcher, the pro-life movement, and free-market economics. There was a grrrl for every flavor: gadgetgrrl .com for the tech-minded, metsgrrl.com for the sports lover. It even made a cameo ("grrrl empowerment") in the Olsen twins' short-lived tween magazine, *mary-kateandashley magazine*.

Needless to say, this was not the revolution. "That was the problem, what the reduction of it to a cute trend never grasped—how emotional and how fragile it was," says Evelyn McDonnell. The hallmarks of riot grrrl—alienated teenagers and punk rock—were still around; the original meanings of "riot grrrl" and "girl power" were simply retired. Besides, with most original riot grrrls pushing their thirties by 2000, a new term to signify their adulthood wouldn't be entirely inappropriate.

"Lady" began to emerge as the third wavers' gender label of choice. (The women of the underground may not have been the forerunners of ladyhood, anyway. In an article on the grrrl-to-lady trend for *Bitch* magazine, Rachel Fudge traces the lady as powerful female figure to Queen Latifah and Monie Love's 1989 duet, "Ladies First.") If anything, "lady" was an unexpected terminology, replacing the vim and vigor of "girl" with more prim-and-proper associations. If riot grrrl had been about taking back the parts of girlhood once deemed unimportant, the same could be said for ladyhood. It may have connoted etiquette and gloves and aristocracy, but it also was reminiscent of being articulate and taken seriously—things that, as riot grrrls aged, they were increasingly aware of as positive values in their own lives, especially in light of the riot grrrl press debacle of the early nineties.

By the late nineties, "lady" was unavoidable in the feminist underground: there was Sleater-Kinney's song "Ballad of a Lady Man" and the queer-feminist record label Mr. Lady, whose co-founder, Kaia Wilson, released an album called *Ladyman*. In

2000, Kathleen Hanna's band Le Tigre, the label's most well-known group, had a song, "LT Tour Theme," that dedicates itself to "the ladies and the fags." That same year, Bratmobile re-formed after a five-year hiatus and put out the album *Ladies, Women, and Girls.* Inga Muscio wrote in *Cunt,* her paean to vulvar reclamation, a "Womanifesto for the Categorical New Freedom Lady" (sample quote: "every time you look in the mirror and your heart races/ because you think/'I'm so fucking rad,'/that's self-protection"). Beyond music, the Ladies Art Revival was a New Jersey–based feminist film distributor, and Miranda July's Joanie 4 Jackie chain letter video project comprised "lady-made" movies.

In 2001, when Fudge wrote her article, she cautioned that "lady" could go the way of "girl": "Words lose their liberating force when adopted by a mainstream far removed from the original moment of creation/reclamation—they become hollow, no longer signifiers of insiderness but rather another element for confusion. Are you a *lady* (wink-wink) or a lady? Only time will tell." But "lady" never was appropriated as a marketing tool or as teenspeak. There were no LADIES RULE T-shirts or Lady brands of lip gloss. The term managed to stay in the community, where it has retained a measure of insider status, although there have always been ladies at the fringe of mass culture: the drag queen Lady Bunny, the pop sensation Lady Gaga, Deee lite's Lady Miss Kier, and the musician Ladyhawke.

Perhaps the locus of the lady boom was Ladyfest, a festival of art made by women and born directly from riot grrrl. When the Experience Music Project organized a retrospective of the movement, many original riot grrrls, who hadn't spoken to the mainstream media since the early nineties, came aboard to give interviews for the show. "When they got together they felt, 'Why end it here?' They were all active as individuals but didn't feel there was a cohesion anymore in terms of activism," Sleater-Kinney's Carrie Brownstein told the *Los Angeles Times.* "They thought, 'Maybe we should do something that's giving people political tools to create culture, not just consume it.'" And in the summer of 2000, in Olympia, Washington, a festival was born. Ladyfest was very clearly part of the punk-rock tradition: the "A" in "lady" was an anarchy symbol.

While more than fifty all- (or mostly) girl bands appeared, Ladyfest was more than a music festival: it contained fashion shows, workshops on topics from basic auto mechanics to gardening to how to organize an orgy, panels on fat oppression and gender socialization in schools, dance parties, and heavy metal karaoke. Ladyfest was by and for women, but it was never meant to be an exclusively female space in the Michigan Womyn's Music Festival vein. The organizers called themselves "self-identified women," which was meant to be more inclusive of trans people. It was even lauded in the mainstream media: *Time* ran an article about the festival called "Olympia Ladystyle." After six days, Ladyfest ended with a $30,000 profit that organizers donated to a rape center and a women's health fund. The message of Ladyfest was so DIY that attendees were explicitly told not to simply anticipate the next time one would be organized in Olympia, but to take from the experience and create a Ladyfest in their own towns. It worked. In the following years, more than one hundred localized manifestations of the festival sprang up on six continents, all with the same blend of girl-centric music, art, and activism.

Ladyfest was proof that even though riot grrrl's era had ended, its ethos was still being lived in the underground. The same women who had once called themselves riot grrrls with pride were still interested in the intersection of punk, feminism, and activism—they just weren't rallied under one moniker any longer. They weren't lying around waiting—most of these bands had been active throughout the nineties—but suddenly, in the Britney age, feminist music sounded good again. Ladyfest was what riot grrrl would have looked like if it had a chance to grow up: organized and political, with a clear message for its community.

Riot grrrl had existed in a minute window of time, and for some girls who had been too young to experience it, Ladyfests were a chance to take part in the movement. Even though the feminist archivist Lizzie Ehrenhalt was in elementary school during riot grrrl's peak, she still longed for it. Simply put, she wanted girls playing music whom she could look up to. She heard Sleater-Kinney's "One More Hour" on a mix tape. "I was like, 'That's it, that's what I was looking for!' But no one was listening to riot grrrl. I tried to get some zines. I was ready to go to riot grrrl meetings!" she says. "I felt like I had just missed it, like everyone had gone home and I had just showed up."

The leap that happened during the girl riot in 1991 was the realization that girls could be just as DIY as boys, emboldening a new generation of creative women. Jennifer Baumgardner points to the women that riot grrrl inspired, citing the filmmaker and writer Miranda July as an example of "people who were really young but doing interesting things and then went on to be really important artists of our generation." She's right; riot grrrl's subsequent iterations and evolutions in bands like Sleater-Kinney won a level of mainstream success on their own terms that riot grrrl never came close to. And with that success, they enjoyed an influence that spanned far beyond what riot grrrl ever achieved.

Sleater-Kinney was a kind of riot grrrl supergroup formed by

Corin Tucker and Carrie Brownstein, former members of the Olympia riot grrrl groups Heavens to Betsy and Excuse 17. It was emblematic of a new crop of acts that shared a certain post-grrrl sensibility, both aesthetically and musically, like Peaches, Chicks on Speed, Le Tigre, the Butchies, Bangs, Erase Errata, Lesbians on Ecstasy, the Blow, and Tracy + the Plastics. Like the riot grrrls, these musicians retained control of their image: they (mostly) stayed on independent labels, played all-ages shows and countless political fund-raisers, and asked other similarly minded (and gendered) bands they liked to tour with them. And many of them became legitimately famous—going from feminist icons to rock icons—and played stadiums. Sleater-Kinney, for example, was the opening act for Pearl Jam in 2003, and their namesake exit off the freeway in Lacey, Washington—an innocuous boulevard lined with strip malls—became something of an indie-rock tourist attraction. Even so, they still resisted the corporate lure, recording for the indie labels Kill Rock Stars and Sub Pop.

But unlike their riot grrrl predecessors, these bands didn't shy away from the mainstream. The Gossip, for example, who had come from the same Olympia milieu as many of the riot grrrl bands, embraced the media in ways their predecessors refused. The band's biggest hit, "Standing in the Way of Control"—about same-sex marriage—went gold in the United Kingdom, and its charismatic singer, Beth Ditto, appeared in British *Vogue* and penned an advice column for *The Guardian*. She found a certain kind of fame after toiling for years in the underground, but it was a Pyrrhic victory: Ditto, who has always called herself fat without apology, also landed on the cover of the *National Enquirer* for her preference for fried chicken and ice cream, labeled one of "Hollywood's Deadliest Diets." (As a response, she's scrawled PUNK ROCK

WILL NEVER DIET on her body during photo shoots.) In 2009, she launched a plus-size clothing line with the British retailer Evans. Her nude appearance on the cover of *NME* in 2007 was met with both jeers and lauds. The magazine's motive for putting her on the cover was obviously to move copies, not advance fat-positive feminism, but it still provided an image of a body type that is rarely seen in the mainstream media. And even though other magazines, like France's *Les Inrockuptibles*, ran the photo for their own covers, it's telling that no American magazines did. For all of Ditto's fame in Europe, she remains an underground figure in the United States. But when Sharon Cheslow saw the image, she remembers thinking, "That's it—riot grrrl is a success. That was the whole idea."

Both Le Tigre and the Gossip got in bed with the mainstream more than Sleater-Kinney dared to, signing to major labels, using big-name producers (like Rick Rubin, and Ric Ocasek from the Cars), and licensing their songs for use in advertisements and on film and television. So did the Donnas, a female quartet from the Bay Area who signed to Atlantic Records in 2001 after years spent on the indie label Lookout Records. They appeared on MTV's popular program *Total Request Live* and posed for fashion spreads. The guitarist Donna R. (in a nod to the Ramones, each member took Donna as her stage name) defended their move. "Women deserve to have a female rock band that is accessible for people. Not everybody lives in towns where they can find independent labels." In the era of online shopping, that argument has less traction, but she does make a point about the hazards of elitism. And the band certainly didn't forget where they came from—they brought a reunited Bratmobile on tour with them as an opening act.

Maybe the dichotomy of mainstream versus underground is itself outdated. It's easy to be strident as a riot grrrl at age twenty-two, all swagger and dogma, full of capital-I Ideals. In the nineties, to lead an aesthetically—and by extension, ethically—pure life, you'd buy limited-edition colored vinyl records instead of CDs, eat a tofu hot dog instead of a turkey sandwich, and go to word-of-mouth shows in living rooms instead of clubs. But looking back, it's easy to find the faults: all that limited-edition vinyl took so much effort (not to mention space) to amass; those tofu dogs are expensive, highly processed, and filled with preservatives; and those house shows were totally elitist. Elitist value judgments about artistic purity were the Achilles heel of the nineties social movements. By the time Le Tigre, the Donnas, and the Gossip were rising to fame, they could flirt with the mainstream and it wasn't considered indie treason.

By 2000—the year that Ladyfest originated and that Sleater-Kinney played in front of thirteen thousand people at the Food Not Bombs twentieth-anniversary concert in San Francisco—I should have felt personal vindication that the music of my adolescence had reached audiences larger than a basement crowd, but by then I was burnt out. There was a certain amount of posturing and claims to purity inherent to indie rock that I was tiring of—an elitism that I had loved when gliding past the cash box at shows, always on the list and secure in my standing in the social hierarchy. But by the end of college, I had been left with a bad taste in my mouth after going to the Olympia summer festival Yoyo-A-Go-Go in 1997 and getting pepper-sprayed because I was standing next to a friend, a boy, who had allegedly made an offensive comment about someone's mother. What he said or whether he actually said anything, I will never know and don't care, because the event felt so emblematic of how much the community had devolved. In 1995, when I was attending the Free to

Fight tour, which combined bands like Sleater-Kinney with self-defense workshops, I never thought that self-defense would be used against me. I somewhat huffily stopped listening to Sleater-Kinney, Le Tigre, and the Gossip for a while. I was glad that they existed, but I needed the distance. I had stopped relating to how angry and earnest they were—I had overdosed on these qualities during my angry and earnest high school and college years. Even listening to their old records or seeing their posters in record shops made me feel guilty, as if the bands could somehow tell I now much preferred listening to Destiny's Child.

I didn't set out to make peace with my riot grrrl past, but in 2002, a friend played me the album *One Beat* in her car, and Sleater-Kinney sounded like they had grown up and moved on as much as I had. The music was made by thirtysomething women who were still frustrated by the status quo—and played louder than ever to prove it—but you could hear that they were living with children and mortgages and standing weekly therapy appointments. Whether or not I personally needed them at that moment in my life, I realized that day that there were countless other girls who did: Sleater-Kinney was bigger than me. As these artists grew up, they took the idea of wanting to live a certain indie ethos and applied it to real—meaning larger, adult, mainstream, busy, complicated—life, and, as a result, their music was more vital than ever. In Sleater-Kinney's case, their 2005 album, *The Woods*, was a departure from their rocking hard "in a girl way." It has a certain finality to it, packed with songs about the complications of success and long-term relationships, ending with the warped lullaby "Night Light," as if they knew all along it would be their last one.

On June 27, 2006, at 3:31 p.m., I wrote an e-mail to my friend

Julianne that simply said, "Sleater-Kinney broke up. My youth is over." I coped by regressing to the pop culture of my high school and college years. Like myself at fifteen, I would lie in bed in the dark, listening to Tori Amos sing "Silent All These Years" over and over (full disclosure: sometimes while tearing up) and watching the Breeders' "Cannonball" video on VH1 Classic and the Sonic Youth concert film *1991: The Year That Punk Broke*. I told all my friends I wanted to start a zine that I would Xerox myself and distribute at punk shows, which I never got around to doing. I went vegan and dressed like Winona Ryder in *Reality Bites*.

I will be the first to admit that I was being more than a little bit dramatic. Maybe because I was a year shy of turning thirty, or possibly because it had been a long time since I had attended a concert in someone's living room, the way I had when I first saw Sleater-Kinney, I was feeling particularly contemplative about what it meant to grow up in the heyday of the angry and earnest female musician. It's a shame that we won't hear what Sleater-Kinney in their forties or fifties would sound like. Then again, as one friend pointed out to me, Sleater-Kinney was together longer than the Beatles.

I saw Sleater-Kinney's raw and tender final New York City concert (one of the last few shows they ever played) and can report that I wasn't alone in my mourning. Alexa Weinstein, a longtime fan, went to their final show, in Portland, and it was nothing short of momentous. "I was glad that as a fan I had stayed with them and they had a big impact on me." She cried and felt like everyone was crying around her. "It really had an end-of-an-era feeling." Connie Wohn, a publicist, was there as well. "It had a finality to it that was sad, but you felt like you were seeing history being made. They create the space and then there's room for more people to get into that space."

As unwelcome as the news of their breakup was, I have to applaud them for quitting while they were still vital. Unfortunately, the breakup of a few of these bands (Le Tigre had also announced an extended hiatus and, by 2005, Ladyfests were on the wane) has been interpreted as one more sign of not just the increasing lack of women in rock, but the death knell of feminism itself. *Salon* called it a "blue moment." *The San Francisco Bay Guardian* wondered, "Where have all the music-making women gone?" At a certain point in their careers, they seemed to tire of discussing the fact that their music was made by women and shied away from calling themselves feminist leaders, ready to let someone else parse the endless discussions of women and rock.

Do these silences indicate a lack of decisive third wave feminist leadership—or just a dated notion that feminists need figureheads? I suspect it has more to do with an unwillingness of mature artists to be defined foremost by their gender. Megan Jasper, the executive vice president of Sleater-Kinney's label, Sub Pop, applauds bands that don't make their gender the center of their career. With Sleater-Kinney, or, earlier, L7, Jasper thought the message was, " 'Yes, we're women, but don't judge us on that. We're musicians and that's how we care to be seen.' I love that about both of those bands. They wanted the music to speak for itself. Hopefully a day will come when there isn't that conversation. I know a lot of people are intent to make that day a reality." At the same time, the idea of getting away from gender has a number of downsides—the primacy put upon being a girl was what drew me to riot grrrl in the first place.

The Le Tigre lyric "Go tell your friends I'm still a feminist/but I won't be coming to your benefit" was about the problem of being a famous feminist whom everyone wants a part of. And maybe carrying the token-feminist mantle more or less alone was too much of a burden for that handful of bands. I wish they hadn't opted out, but in my more optimistic moments I think the lesson is that perhaps more aging leaders in music should take their cue and gracefully step aside. (And I wonder if the feminist movement in general—where a parallel debate has raged since the deaths of legendary women like Betty Friedan, over who the next generation of leaders is, and whether we even need one—might learn a lesson here.) The demise of these key bands has left a gaping void, but I also hope that will encourage a new generation of leaders to step up.

Maybe the true legacy of Sleater-Kinney and of riot grrrl has been the creation of a new generation of musicians. Corin Tucker once said, "We just want to say that we're not here to fuck the band. We are the band." Riot grrrls set out not just to normalize listening to bands with girls in them, but to encourage girls to create music themselves. On the Gossip's MySpace page, they encourage fans to "pick up a guitar and start your own band!" adding, "Perfection is not real."

The desire to be perfect, while not unique to girls, is a persistent hurdle that often stops girls from feeling like they could be legitimate performers. In 2003, a yearlong Duke University study found that its own undergraduate women felt the need to be "effortlessly perfect," combining beauty, intellect, success, style, and a slender body without looking like they were even trying. (The report also mentioned that "women who do flout the norms often remove themselves from the social mainstream, whether voluntarily or not.") The Blow's Khaela Maricich was "too square for riot grrrl, too artsy for Lilith, and too old for the Spice Girls"; nonetheless, she benefited from the make-it-up-as-you-go-along ethos that ran rampant at the Evergreen State College. She had never thought of herself as a musician, but played for the first time at a friend's talent show her sophomore year, accompanied by her brother's ukulele. It was scary but satisfying. "My experience of being a girl is that you don't want to show off in front of people unless you really know what you're doing," she says. "That's a huge dividing line between girls and boys. Guys just do it without thinking. They're so balls out, they just keep throwing shit out there."

Maricich's fans love her because she is a girl and sings about the experience openly. "I acknowledge what it's like to be a person with feelings. I feel like that is what girls respond to me with. I can hear their voices singing along, the girls in the audience, and that confidence passes through me and I'm handing it back over. They'll come up to me and say, 'I totally know what you mean, I know what you're feeling.'"

The idea of girls simply picking up an instrument and starting a band—and that being normal—is, after all, a relatively new concept. Joan Jett, who was in a teen all-girl band, the Runaways, in the seventies, has become such an icon of independence and self-confidence for Gen X and Y women—for her songs, her general badass vibe, and the untethered way she's seemed to live her life—that WWJJD: WHAT WOULD JOAN JETT DO? T-shirts are sold online. "One of the goals of the Runaways was to make it normal for a girl to write and play rock and roll and sweat onstage," Jett told *Billboard* magazine. It wasn't a concern voiced only by women. In an interview with *Rolling Stone* in the mid-eighties, the former Van Halen frontman David Lee Roth shared his thoughts about the state of women and music thusly: "What if a little girl picked up a guitar and said 'I wanna be a rock star'? Nine times out of ten her parents would never allow her to do it. We don't have so many lead guitar women, not because women don't have the ability to play the instrument, but because they're locked up, taught to be something else." Even cemented in his hard-rock view of the universe, Diamond Dave was right; to be a girl who wanted to play music was to choose an uphill battle against the status quo.

In the musical underground, some of the most legendary bands had had female instrumentalists who played alongside men, like Georgia Hubley of Yo La Tengo, Bridget Cross of Unrest, Kim Gordon of Sonic Youth, Kim Deal of the Pixies, Heather Lewis from Beat Happening, Kira Roessler from Black Flag, Naomi Yang of Galaxie 500, Tina Weymouth of Talking Heads, and Moe Tucker of the Velvet Underground. That they functioned primarily as instrumentalists rather than lead singers proved that girls could be in bands, breaking up the typical all-boy rock equation or the slightly more common trope of male instrumentalists flanking a pretty and charismatic female frontwoman—Blondie perhaps being the most notable example (which isn't inherently bad but something I've often felt a bit of distrust toward).

Women as creators of rock music have changed considerably in the past generation or two. Pop culture of the eighties and nineties helped propel girls toward playing music. Quirky girls were heroines: any character played by Winona Ryder, or the women of John Hughes's teen oeuvre, notably in his screenplay for the film *Some Kind of Wonderful*. In it, Mary Stuart Masterson plays the cute, boyish drummer—who still gets the guy in the end. The movie gave many girls hope that they could reside at the bottom of high school's social hierarchy, have interests that weren't classically feminine, speak their minds, and precisely for those very reasons, attract men. The overwhelming DIY aesthetic of the era, which encouraged everyone to pick up an instrument, regardless of one's expertise or lack thereof, also helped inspire girls who might otherwise have been too intimidated. "People who couldn't play anyway—boys—were doing it, and once that opened up, there was no reason not to be a girl and do it," Liz Phair told *New York* magazine.

One of the great indie-rock clichés is the token female bass player, never taken seriously because the bass is considered an easy instrument to get a grip on. And even once in the band, female bassists could still struggle to prove themselves worthy; Talking Heads', singer, David Byrne, famously made Tina Weymouth audition twice for her spot in the band: once to join and again years later after they got a contract with Sire Records, even though her catchy, minimal bass lines had already become a trademark of their music and she would later go on to write and produce some of the band's songs. But women's place is becoming more normalized. "When I first started playing music in a band in the late eighties, it was much more unusual for women to be playing an instrument in a band; now it's not unusual at all," says Naomi Yang of Galaxie 500 and Damon and Naomi, who was inspired to play bass after spending hours during architecture school listening to Joy Division and New Order—and loving Peter Hook's bass lines. But the novelty of the girl in the band has gradually worn off. "When I'm on tour now, there's at least one woman every night at the clubs, playing or working," says Kori Gardner-Hammel of the band Mates of State. "Ten years ago, I would go on tour and I would be the only woman I'd see the whole time."

In musical instruction, guitars, drums, and brass instruments are still largely played by boys. While the days of girls being automatically steered toward "feminine" (higher pitch, more delicate) instruments may be waning, girls still predominate among flute and harp players. How these gender associations came to be is up for debate: the size of the instrument (although pianos and harps are huge) is a factor, as are its traditional uses—drums and brass instruments have long been used in the military. Learned gender behaviors are another barrier to women picking up rock instruments. "Classical music is the epitome of Western cultural values because women musicians are seated and controlled," says Sharon Cheslow, herself a guitar player. "One of the reasons why the playing field of music hasn't equalized as it has in fine arts or films is because women being on a stage and performing with an instrument is in some way threatening on a larger societal level. One aspect of rock and punk that was very noticeable was seeing women using their bodies in ways that expressed the body's power." When the musician and writer Alex Weinstein learned to play the drums, it was the physicality of it that was the most terrifying part. She not only had to learn to let herself literally make noise, but to allow her stomach to hang out, which is a difficult thing for any girl who grew up reading teen-magazine diet and exercise tips. "Drumming is crazy. You make faces, you have to pound with your whole body. You have to sit with your legs spread." For people not accustomed to seeing women act that way, that alone is enough to threaten the status quo.

A 2008 study of sixteen-year-olds in England and Wales by the Institute of Education found that girls are much more fluid about taking up these so-called male instruments like drums and guitar, while boys just aren't as willing to learn feminine instruments. Of course, the vast majority of school-age boys aren't growing up listening to the flute or the harp (perhaps the acclaim of harpist/musical savant/critical darling Joanna Newsom will help correct that), the way that girls are exposed to guitar or bass. "Ten years ago, statistics showed that 96 percent of the instruments purchased were for men," Gibson's chief executive Henry Juszkiewicz told the

Associated Press in 2007. But with the influence of hugely popular instrument-based video games like Guitar Hero and Rock Band (both of which offer pink "guitar" controllers aimed at girl gamers), playing at making rock music is a standard part of adolescence—male or female. Guitar makers have taken note, creating models directed at girls, like the Daisy Rock Guitars line, Gibson's Les Paul Goddess, and Fender's Hello Kitty model. The fact that marketing to girls automatically equates with the color pink, flowers, goddesses, and anthropomorphic cats is, well, another battle.

Men still set the standards for what is considered greatness, instrument-playing being no exception. So it comes as no surprise that so many successful or ambitious women in bands play down their gender, in order to compete as equals. Who wants to be good "for a girl"? "I was confused when people would say, 'You're such a good guitar player.' If you saw a really good female piano or violin player, would you be surprised? There's this cultural attachment to a guy wanking on his guitar," says the solo musician Marnie Stern, whose virtuosic ability to shred on the guitar has been central to much of what's been written about her. "I don't like that there's separation there. I wondered if I weren't a woman, would people be as attracted to my record? That's why I'm not attracted to the girls' club." She was featured alongside Sleater-Kinney's Carrie Brownstein and the acoustic player Kaki King in an article in *The New York Times* on female guitar heroines of indie rock. Regardless of whether she felt conflicted about her inclusion, it was one of the few articles to discuss the importance of women playing guitar (and it did net Stern positive feedback from other girls who were inspired by her).

If any lesson was learned from riot grrrl, it's that the relationship between women musicians and the press is a complicated one. It's difficult for journalists to highlight the experience of girls playing in bands without further tokenizing them. "In one interview they asked how we'd want to be portrayed," says Mary Pearson of High Places. "I said that anything is fine as long as it doesn't say boy-girl duo." The male members of Rainer Maria had a joke about "the Caithlin question" aimed at their singer Caithlin De Marrais: What's it like to be a girl in a band? The musician and DJ Shayla Hason describes the sensation of reading an article about a female instrumentalist whose gender isn't her defining trait as "like a movie where there's a gay character and the plot doesn't revolve around them being gay."

One possible solution is to simply recruit women to start playing music at a younger and more impressionable age. "I wish I had looked at Barbie and the Rockers when I was nine and said, Let's start a band," says the writer and musician Erin Walter. "How cool would I have been if I started a band when I was nine? It astounds me that it didn't dawn on me to be in a band till twenty-five."

The first Rock 'n' Roll Camp for Girls began in the early millennium in that bastion of girl righteousness, Portland, Oregon. The camp's founder, Misty McElroy, herself a former roadie, organized it as the community service component of her women's studies degree at Portland State University. (Summer camps targeting young women who are at a high risk for poor self-esteem aren't just the domain of budding rock musicians. In Vermont, there's a camp called Rosie's Girls—named for the iconic Rosie the Riveter—that teaches teens skills like welding, electrical wiring, auto repair, carpentry, and firefighting. Nomy Lamm, who wrote a classic riot-grrrl-era zine called *I'm So Fucking Beautiful*, was involved in a fat-positive, trans-positive group called Phat Camp in Chicago.)

At the Rock 'n' Roll Camp for Girls, budding musicians from

the ages of eight to eighteen flocked to the camp from all over the world to learn to play the instrument of their choice, form a band, and play a concert—all in the space of one week. It was so popular that a sister branch, Willie Mae Rock Camp, opened in New York City in 2005. As with Ladyfest, women inspired by the camps organized versions in their own cities, so that in the ensuing years, so many camps formed across the United States, Europe, and South America that they formed the Girls Rock Camp Alliance. The reaction from most women who hear about the camp is envy that they didn't have it when they were growing up. For that very reason, the first Ladies Rock Camp (of course it's "ladies"!) debuted in Portland in 2004.

I've spent a number of days at the Willie Mae camp over the last few summers talking to campers. The camp is held at a Brooklyn high school transformed temporarily into rock-and-roll high school, with M.I.A. songs blasting in the hallway. The girls are equal parts alienated and elated, and it shows in their outfits of sparkly blue Converse sneakers and studded leather cuffs and braces. In a 2007 songwriting workshop, where "Pre-chorus, Verse, Chorus" was written on the board, groups of junior-high-age girls with band names like Roadkill Rewind were brainstorming lyrics. "What rhymes with 'fishies'?" one asked. The girls were cheering and cracking up at each lyric. The band coach—the rock camp's version of a camp counselor—offered them some truly helpful commentary on the craft of songwriting. "Can you figure out less syllables without losing meaning in the story?"

The camps' girls-rule aesthetic is reminiscent of the Spice Girls, but the dedication to teaching campers how to change their own lives and the world around them—marrying pop and politics—is pure riot grrrl. And if there's any question of the debt the camps owe to that movement, the Portland and New York camps' programs have articles penned by Tobi Vail and Carrie Brownstein. (The riot grrrl influence hasn't been unilaterally welcomed. In the summer of 2008, a mother angered by the "graphic violent imagery and lyrics" of a Bikini Kill tape sent home with her eight-year-old from the Portland camp made the news, but that was also proof that the camp's reach far exceeded the kind of culturally privileged parents who would delight in their daughters discovering punk while still in grammar school.)

It is hard not to cry during rock camp. I kept tearing up and hiding my face in my notebook, afraid that the girls would think I was hopelessly corny, the way I thought my own mother was when she'd cry during my ballet recitals. I finally succumbed to public weeping while attending the amazing and inspirational end-of-camp showcase concert, where a band called the Exploding Amps sang, "Don't be afraid/Let your energy be free/Let's be whoever we wanna be/Life is too short/to be fake/so be yourself/for goodness sake." Or there was Disturbed Disney's paean to Alice in Wonderland's inherent loneliness. "Poor Alice had no one to help her deal," but they conclude that she has to stand up for herself: "Locked talking doors with no exit/Feeling trapped and alone/She wasn't going down without a fight." The Portland rock camp inspired a documentary, *Girls Rock!* Watching the campers change so much over the course of a week, Arne Johnson, one of the filmmakers, noted, "Part of what's amazing about rock camp is how little it takes for girls to blossom. Separate them from boys and give them instruments. They're not getting mixed messages for once."

To campers like Laura Walters, who was fifteen when she appeared in the *Girls Rock!* documentary, the question of how the camp has changed her life has become something of a cliché.

"How many times has someone asked me this, and how many different answers have I given?" she says, practically yawning. Instead, she tells me that reading about the camp in the now defunct teen magazine *YM* and a viewing of *The Matrix: Reloaded* with her dad are the two main things that helped change her musical life. She discovered Rage Against the Machine on the *Matrix* sound track, which became her gateway to other bands. "I tend to jump around and dance a lot," she says. "My vocals themselves aren't beautiful; in fact, one of my friends listened to a recording of my band's song and told me that it sounds like I'm just shouting. But you know what??" she writes in an e-mail. "I AM just shouting!!! Shouting is fun and I really don't want to apologize for it." Alexis Dittrich, who was a camper in Portland in 2002 and a counselor in 2003, wrote an essay for the program about her band Glitter in the Skin's showcase performance, where they decided to forget their nerves and wear matching glitter zip-up unisuits. "When I came to the Rock 'n' Roll Camp for Girls, I was scared to don my glitter unisuit. Now I'm terrified of just the opposite. No matter how far I venture into the unknown, or what challenges I face, I will always have the drive to put passion into action. I will always have glitter on my skin."

Some of the bands formed during camp, like Blübird in Portland and Magnolia in New York, have stayed together and continue to write songs, playing shows outside of the showcase and releasing music. Zora Sicher and Hugo Orozco of Magnolia went to the inaugural New York session in 2005 and attended again in 2006, and told a *Newsweek* reporter that they intend to go until they're eighteen, and then become counselors. Both of them have the benefit of cool parents with excellent taste—Orozco's took her to see queercore bands like the Butchies, which, in turn, inspired her to play music. At a Brooklyn concert, when I asked if they listened to groups like the Spice Girls, they gave me a look like I was a billion years old and said that sometimes when they go to band practice they'll turn on a pop radio station, admitting that some of the music gets stuck in their heads.

Sicher and Orozco were both born in the mid-nineties. They were playing shows and getting feted by the press at the age of eleven. And they're not the only ones. Sisters Chloe and Asya of the band Smoosh—they don't give out their last names—released their first album when Asya was twelve and Chloe was ten. It seems that the average age of the female rebel rocker icon has decreased, from seventies punk femmes like Debbie Harry and Patti Smith in their late twenties and early thirties, to the riot grrrls in their teens and early twenties, to this new wave of girls who aren't even in their teens yet when they form bands. They look completely natural onstage too. While they may not be making any overt political statements (I was in fact disappointed while interviewing Chloe from Smoosh when she said, "I don't really think about feminism too much. I don't really think of myself as that"), they might not need to be as overt as previous generations, where a woman getting onstage was a statement in itself. And in that sense, what Smoosh did was utterly political, whether intended or not.

6

GIRL POWER

I t's the night before Valentine's Day 2008 and I'm at the Spice Girls reunion concert at the Izod Arena in New Jersey. Though the Spice Girls themselves have declared that this reunion is "not about the money," they are said to be making over $100 million on the tour. Simon Fuller, the manager they fired at the height of their career and who now manages several of their solo careers, is back as well. But is girl power?

The hundreds of people at Port Authority Bus Station in Manhattan, waiting for the bus that would take us to New Jersey, showed that I wasn't the only one who was curious to see what had come of it. The line seemed composed entirely of girls in their twenties and thirties and their gay male best friends. There really seemed to be no straight men around—it was kind of a safe space not just for girls, but also for gay boys who surely had some kind of awakening singing along to "Wannabe" in their bedrooms.

I'm sitting in the upper level with two friends, eating a Carvel ice cream sundae for dinner and watching the crowd. Even though I'm dying to see Ginger, Baby, Sporty, Scary, and Posh—especially Posh—in the flesh, the crowd itself fascinates me. There are girls in their late teens and early twenties who grew up with the Spice Girls; older women and gay men who all seem to be there, like me, as cultural tourists; and massive groups of young girls, proving that the Spices' infectious music is evergreen. There is a lot of screaming and a few sections do the wave. Those with sparkly makeup and glow sticks surely outnumber those of us without.

There are girls dressed like the Spices, or girls just dressed in matching outfits (black leggings with neon minidresses; black mini-dresses with neon leggings). Roberto Cavalli, the official costume designer of the reunion tour, has elaborate ads on the Jumbo-trons, but everywhere I look are girls sporting homemade Spice Girls T-shirts, which seems charmingly subversive and DIY, though that doesn't stop the merch tables from being bombarded with people. I buy a set of buttons that say GIRL POWER and WANNABE and a tote bag that declares WHAT I WANT WHAT I REALLY REALLY WANT in neon, rainbow block letters.

The Spices finally come on and the whole show is a spectacle of male dancers being walked on diamante leashes, the girls gy-rating on candy-striped stripper poles (to the "Let's Get It On"–lite of "2 Become 1"), and some pantomimed bullfighting. The conceit of Spices as seductresses is played out in each of their solo songs: Posh—who gets by far the most cheers from the crowd—goes first and doesn't even pretend to sing, but struts down a run-way to "Vogue," seducing the paparazzi or maybe just herself. Baby sings a Petula Clark–ish song while wearing a minidress and doing the frug. Sporty, who never made the most convincing seductress (of men, at least), sings her solo hit "I Turn to You," and Ginger does "It's Raining Men." Scary goes for high camp when she sings "Are You Gonna Go My Way" while brandishing a whip and simulating a blow job on an obviously gay man who looks delighted to be a part of the ridiculous scene.

But lest we forget that the Spice Girls have grown and matured in the last ten years into Spice Women, there's a montage of their photos with their own kids. By the time confetti rained down over the audience during "Spice World" and the girls came out dressed in silver sequins, holding hands and striding down the center of the stage, I whispered to my friend Kara, "I refuse to believe the rumors that they don't really get along."

I can see how pining for the Spice Girls of all things seems like nostalgia at its worst, but their concert felt like one night where girls could be strong and frivolous and free to wear lip gloss and bare their midriffs and no one was overthinking it. It surely wasn't feminism in action—there were certainly no political agendas being pushed or community organizing being done, and I'm sure Posh's spindly thighs were doing nothing for anyone's body issues—but it was thousands of girls in one place simply celebrating the state of being a girl.

I'm not sure there's a cultural equivalent for guys, especially not heterosexual ones. There is pop music made by guys (boy bands, teen R&B sensations), and there is plenty of music steeped in machismo and virility, but no songs marketed to teen boys expressly about the state of being a teenage boy. Perhaps boys don't need to be reminded of their own power, ergo no boy-power anthems. But the music of girl power has found a very public boy fanbase on the online video sharing site YouTube. Countless teen boys can be found singing and dancing along to "Wannabe" and "Girls Just Want to Have Fun," all of whom are poking fun at the songs but also reveling in their glory.

There's a clip of a bearded hipster boy lip syncing Bikini Kill's "Rebel Girl" in the comfort of his own home that I'm particularly drawn to. I've watched it dozens of times and, after each viewing, I like to imagine what the impact of riot grrrl would have been like with today's Internet. It definitely would have eased the task of finding fellow grrrls to bond with, especially ones who lived in far-flung locales; in the pre-Internet era, being a teen with esoteric interests—vintage clothes, insidery bands, arcane knowledge of foreign cinema—usually meant spending a lot of time alone. But now even writing in one's diary, that most solitary of pastimes, has with online journals become a public act. We're so used to seeing teens' staged provocative photos of themselves, the press wouldn't be nearly as excited over a group of girls who scrawled RAPE on their bellies with Sharpie markers. With an army of grrrl bloggers, the media blackout wouldn't have hurt the movement nearly as much: bands would have been able to connect directly with their fans, girls could have bashed press coverage on discussion boards, musicians could have released new songs directly from their own websites. As someone from a pre-Internet adolescence, however, I believe virtual connections can never entirely take the place of real-life connections. I'm reminded of the Le Tigre song whose chorus beseeches us to "Get off the internet/I'll meet you in the streets/Get off the internet/Destroy the right wing."

A few months after the Spice Girls reunion and a night spent watching Liz Phair singing the entirety of *Exile in Guyville*, I went to my first riot grrrl tribute concert. The band played at the premiere party for a documentary about the Gits. The music was a fitting tribute, made all the more moving because that night happened to fall on the fifteenth anniversary of the singer Mia Zapata's death. The band played Hole and Bikini Kill and L7—the semantics of what bands were and weren't rightfully riot grrrl were thankfully cast aside for the night—to an audience that included Kathleen Hanna, Allison Wolfe, and a lot of girls who, like me, looked like they were caught in a riot grrrl reverie.

I didn't snap out of it. In the days following I couldn't stop thinking about my obsession with that era. Fifteen years after I had first heard Phair's *Exile* and Bikini Kill's *Pussy Whipped* and the Breeder's *Last Splash*, I wondered why the nineties girl bands held such a place of importance in my own life. Riot grrrl sent shockwaves through nineties music of all genres, changing both feminist discourse and pop culture. But by the time nascent grrrls in far-flung suburbs found out about the movement, it was already over, but it survived as a catalyst for turning women into creators. Its core message lived on, shapeshifting its way through the nineties and beyond, from the Spice Girls and Miley Cyrus foregrounding female friendship to Christina Aguilera and Beth Ditto railing against the patriarchy. As a result, girls were able to see themselves in the cultural forefront as never before, whether they identified with Courtney Love or Avril Lavigne, Liz Phair or Britney Spears. In the end, performers once dismissed as solely harmful to the cause of women—the Britneys of the world—might also be seen as helpful, as their stories lay bare some of the manipulation and tribulations that women are often exposed to. That's girl power's true legacy.

What I miss the most from that era is the celebration of women rocking out live onstage, especially in the current era of online video, where watching your favorite band is easy, but the volume and viscerality of the live experience is lost in translation. And while there are plenty of girls starting rock bands and taking up the guitar, guitar-based rock is no longer the primary vehicle for exploring musical creativity; some of the musicians I listen to the most these days are not confined to one genre, infusing pop, dance music, and hip-hop with messages of girl power. Rebellion does not have to be about being loud. I understand that music, like feminism, has to reinvent itself if it's going to remain vital to each new generation. But I do miss the more overt feminism and sense of purpose that riot grrrl had. "Bringing music back to the political sphere is powerful," says Lois Maffeo, "but maybe music did its job already." I think, however, that music hasn't yet fulfilled its feminist destiny and that girl power has a long way to go.

Girl power recognizes that not everything is pure: it delights in ambiguous gray areas. It's not just about testing out your own relationship to feminism, but about finding your identity in the world. But girl power's "do-it-yourself" message of "you can do anything" is a powerful entrée to feminism, especially because its simplicity brings in the very young. If the third wave was in part about reclaiming a sense of the purely feminine in feminism, then we need to look toward the fourth wave to not let that get out of control to the point where we forget how we got here. Girl power is a way station, not an endpoint, and a gateway, I hope, to a more profound equality of the sexes.

There is still so much for young women to accomplish, even in countries that have reaped the rewards of second and third wave feminism: equal pay, less body obsession, sexual politics without double standards, and political parity, to name a few goals. But this current generation of girls has unprecedented tools at its disposal—the benefit of advanced networking technology, female role models in all fields, a history of feminist achievements to learn from, equal opportunities in school, and, of course, an amazing catalog of music as inspiration. Girl power has planted the philosophical seeds that will enact a change in global worldview, making these goals look reachable and finally commonplace. When girls in their bedrooms around the world recognize that they're connected—via the Internet, their experiences, their love of the same pop culture—they will see that the flaw in girl power is to fixate on the individual; real power will come when they decide to band together.

SELECTED BIBLIOGRAPHY AND FILMOGRAPHY

Arnold, Gina. *Route 666: On the Road to Nirvana* (New York: St. Martin's Press, 1993).

Aronson, Pamela. "Feminists or 'Postfeminists'?: Young Women's Attitudes Toward Feminism and Gender Relations," *Gender and Society*, December 2003.

Azzerad, Michael. *Our Band Could Be Your Life: Scenes from the American Indie Underground, 1981–1991* (New York: Little, Brown, 2001).

Bauer, Carlene. "The Riot Quiets," *Salon*, July 17, 2006.

Baumgardner, Jennifer, and Amy Richards. *Manifesta: Young Women, Feminism, and the Future* (New York: Farrar, Straus and Giroux, 2000).

Bayton, Mavis. *Frock Rock: Women Performing Popular Music* (New York: Oxford University Press, 1998).

Bellafante, Ginia. "Is Feminism Dead?" *Time*, June 29, 1998.

Douglas, Susan. *Where the Girls Are: Growing Up Female with the Mass Media* (New York: Three Rivers Press, 1995).

Brumberg, Joan Jacobs. *The Body Project: An Intimate History of American Girls* (New York: Vintage, 1998).

Carpenter, Sue. "This Lady's More Riot Grrrl Than Lilith," *Los Angeles Times*, August 7, 2000.

SELECTED BIBLIOGRAPHY AND FILMOGRAPHY

Carson, Mina, Tisa Lewis, and Susan M. Shaw. *Girls Rock!: Fifty Years of Women Making Music* (Lexington: University Press of Kentucky, 2004).

Chebatoris, Jac. "So You Want to Be a (Grrrl) Rock and Roll Star," *Newsweek*, January 26, 2007.

Chideya, Farai. "Revolution, Girl Style," *Newsweek*, November 23, 1992.

Chun, Kimberly. "A Band of Sisters," *The San Francisco Bay Guardian*, July 18, 2006.

Crossroads. Dir. Tamra Davis. Paramount Pictures, 2002.

Don't Need You: The Herstory of Riot Grrrl. Dir. Kerri Koch. Urban Cowgirl Productions, 2006.

Gaar, Gillian. *She's a Rebel: The History of Women in Rock and Roll* (Seattle: Seal Press, 1992).

Gilligan, Carol. *In a Different Voice: Psychological Theory and Women's Development* (Cambridge, MA: Harvard University Press, 1993).

Gilmore, Mikal. "The Madonna Mystique," *Rolling Stone*, September 10, 2007.

Goldman, Debra. "The Consumer Republic," *Adweek*, November 17, 1997.

Gottlieb, Joanne, and Gayle Wald. "Smells Like Teen Spirit: Revolution and Women in Independent Rock" in *Microphone Fiends: Youth Music and Youth Culture*, ed. Andrew Ross and Tricia Rose (New York: Routledge, 1994).

Faludi, Susan. *Backlash: The Undeclared War Against American Women* (New York: Crown, 1991).

Feigenbaum, Anna. "Remapping the Resonances of Riot Grrrl" in *Interrogating Postfeminism: Gender and the Politics of Popular Culture*, ed. Diane Negra and Yvonne Tasker (Durham: Duke University Press, 2007).

France, Kim. "Feminism, Amplified," *New York*, June 3, 1996.

———. "Grrrls at War," *Rolling Stone*, July 8, 1993.

Girls Rock! Dir. Arne Johnson and Shane King. Shadow Distribution, 2008.

Harris, John. "Girl Power as Anachronism," *The Guardian*, July 17, 2006.

Heath, Chris. "Fiona: The Caged Bird Sings," *Rolling Stone*, January 28, 1998.

Hermes, Will. "Guitar Heroes, Make That Heroines, in Indie Rock," *The New York Times*, March 11, 2007.

Hopper, Jessica. *The Girls' Guide to Rocking: How to Start a Band, Book Gigs, and Get Rolling to Rock Stardom* (New York: Workman Publishing Company, 2009).

Jervis, Lisa, and Andi Zeisler. *BITCHfest: Ten Years of Cultural Criticism from the Pages of* Bitch *Magazine* (New York: Farrar, Straus and Giroux, 2006).

Josie and the Pussycats. Dir. Harry Elfont and Deborah Kaplan. Universal Pictures, 2001.

Ladies and Gentlemen, The Fabulous Stains. Dir. Lou Adler. Paramount Pictures, 1981.

Lamb, Sharon, and Lyn Mikel Brown. *Packaging Girlhood: Rescuing Our Daughters from Marketers' Schemes* (New York: St. Martin's Griffin, 2007).

Levy, Ariel. *Female Chauvinist Pigs: Women and the Rise of Raunch Culture* (New York: Free Press, 2005).

Love, Courtney. *Dirty Blonde: The Diaries of Courtney Love* (New York: Faber and Faber, 2006).

Marcus, Greil. *The Shape of Things to Come: Prophecy and the American Voice* (New York: Farrar, Straus and Giroux, 2006).

McClary, Susan. *Feminine Endings: Music, Gender, and Sexuality* (Minneapolis: University of Minnesota Press, 2002).

McDonnell, Evelyn. *Mamarama: A Memoir of Sex, Kids, and Rock 'n' Roll* (Cambridge, MA: Da Capo Press, 2007).

McFarland, Melanie. "Don't Hate Me Because I'm Powerful—Girl Power; It's on the Streets and in the Stores. Who's Really Buying It?" *The Seattle Times*, August 2, 1998.

Meshbah, Mariam. "Spice Girl Power: Marketers Really, Really Like It," *Kidscreen*, September 1, 1998.

Monem, Nadine, ed. *Riot Grrrl: Revolution Girl Style Now!* (London: Black Dog Publishing, 2007).

O'Brien, Lucy. *Madonna: Like an Icon* (New York: HarperCollins, 2007).

Orenstein, Peggy. "What's Wrong with Cinderella?" *The New York Times Magazine*, December 24, 2006.

Pipher, Mary. *Reviving Ophelia: Saving the Selves of Adolescent Girls* (New York: Riverhead Trade, 2005).

Powers, Ann. "Fiona Apple: Trying Something New, Trying Something Mellow," *The New York Times*, October 25, 1997.

———. "No Longer Rock's Playthings," *The New York Times*, February 14, 1993.

———. "When Women Venture Forth," *The New York Times*, October 9, 1994.

SELECTED BIBLIOGRAPHY AND FILMOGRAPHY

Press, Joy. "Notes on Girl Power," *The Village Voice*, September 23, 1997.

Raha, Maria. *Cinderella's Big Score: Women of the Punk and Indie Underground* (Seattle: Seal Press, 2004).

Report of the APA Task Force on the Sexualization of Girls (Washington, D.C.: American Psychological Association, 2007).

Reynolds, Simon. "Belting Out That Most Unfeminine Emotion," *The New York Times*, February 9, 1992.

Reynolds, Simon, and Joy Press. *The Sex Revolts: Gender, Rebellion, and Rock 'n' Roll* (Cambridge, MA: Harvard University Press, 1995).

Rhodes, Lisa L. *Electric Ladyland: Women and Rock Culture* (Philadelphia: University of Pennsylvania Press, 2005).

Riot Grrrl Retrospective. Experience Music Project, 1999.

Rosen, Jody. "Mean Grrrl," *Slate*, May 9, 2007.

Schlit, Kristen. "A Little Too Ironic: The Appropriation and Packaging of Riot Grrrl Politics by Mainstream Female Musicians," *Popular Music and Society*, November 1, 2003.

Schoemer, Karen. "The Selling of Girl Power," *Newsweek*, December 29, 1997.

Schou, Solvej. "Making a Play for Girls," Associated Press, March 13, 2007.

Snead, Elizabeth. "Feminist Riot Grrrls Don't Just Wanna Have Fun," *USA Today*, August 7, 1992.

Spencer, Lauren. "Grrrls Only: From the Youngest, Toughest Daughters of Feminism—Self Respect You Can Rock To," *The Washington Post*, January 3, 1993.

Spice World. Dir. Bob Spiers. Columbia Pictures, 1996.

Spin. "The Girl Issue," November 1997.

Wald, Gayle. "Just a Girl? Rock Music, Feminism, and the Cultural Construction of Female Youth," *Signs: Journal of Women in Culture and Society*, 1998.

Walker, Rebecca. *To Be Real: Telling the Truth and Changing the Face of Feminism* (New York: Anchor, 1995).

Wallis, Claudia. "Women Face the '90s," *Time*, December 4, 1989.

White, Emily. "Revolution Girl Style Now" in *Rock She Wrote: Women Write About Rock, Pop, and Rap*, ed. Evelyn McDonnell and Ann Powers (New York: Dell Publishers, 1995).

SELECTED BIBLIOGRAPHY AND FILMOGRAPHY

Whiteley, Sheila, ed. *Sexing the Groove: Popular Music and Gender* (New York: Routledge, 1997).

Williams, Mary Elizabeth. "Tween Bees," *Salon*, February 12, 2008.

Wolf, Naomi. *The Beauty Myth: How Images of Beauty Are Used Against Women* (New York: Harper Perennial, 2002).

ACKNOWLEDGMENTS

I couldn't have written this book without the support of Denise Oswald. I can't think of another editor who would have not only agreed that a trip to a feminist separatist music festival was necessary research for a book on girl power, but volunteered to drive me there, pack me a mess kit, and brave the communal showers by my side. I am so grateful to everyone at FSG who worked on the book: Kathy Daneman, Jessica Ferri, and, particularly, Mitzi Angel and Chantal Clarke.

Thanks to Sarah Lazin, for being supportive of this project since the beginning, and to Melissa Flashman, for loving the nineties as much as I do. Writing this book gave me newfound appreciation for my parents, who, I am just now realizing, were surprisingly lenient about letting their teenage daughter attend concerts on school nights.

I want to thank everyone—fans, musicians, label founders, zine editors, deep thinkers—who sat for an interview; your stories had a huge influence on me. I owe all my friends for their support, especially those who made me their plus-ones, read early drafts, let me stay in their guest rooms, or gave me memorable pep talks: Miriam Bale, Jona Bechtolt, Jon Caramanica, Windy Chien, Rebecca Willa Davis, Elisabeth Donnelly, Claire L. Evans, Emily Gould, Anitra Grisales, Shayla Hason, Sheri Hood, Kara Jesella, Melissa Laux, Joon Lee, Kathryn Lewis, Marianna Ritchey, Doree Shafrir, Holly Siegel, Luke Stiles, Lauren Waterman, Tae Won Yu, and Andi Zeisler.

INDEX

INDEX

INDEX

INDEX

INDEX

INDEX

INDEX